GLASS CUBE
STRATEGY

Corporate Transparency with Integrity
for Trustworthy Enterprise

David Lyback

Image credit: Cover 3D-art named "*27 perfect prisms*" is an original rendering made by the author, using open-source software Blender2.76a to produce a view of an idealistic glass cube with internal prisms. The physical graphics method chosen was raytraced transparency refractions with up to 7 inter-reflections, with Fresnel effect and specular highlights. The material of the prisms had full clarity complete gloss, and the raytracing applied Cook-Torrance shading. Scene light sources were one high-energy point emitter and two weaker, additional spotlights.

Additional material:
www.GlassCubeStrategy.com

ISBN-10: 1519628005
ISBN-13: 978-1519628008

Contents

《》

Preface

Openness continues its slow, victorious spread in good business practice worldwide.

Although shameful exceptions of corruption, greed, and sheer incompetence will continue to make headlines for centuries to come, the majority of firms follow a legal and ethical path where good behavior and a transparent attitude makes economic sense[1].

Some direct problems caused by insufficient openness are: weakened customer trust, staff demotivation, and investor skepticism. These three serious drawbacks transforms into reduced economic performance for that corporation, maybe not instantly, but certainly over time, in a well-functioning and competitive market.

---

[1]Advocated lucidly 2003 in *The Naked Corporation* (Ticoll and Tapscott, 2014).

On the more extreme end of the scale, corruption and outright scams should be promptly hunted down with appropriate regulatory oversight and law enforcement, and scammers expelled from the field. Opacity helps them to hide easily.

Like most people, I hate corruption: how it dilutes resources and enrich some persons for all the wrong reasons. It also upsets me when bandits play shop only to steal from ordinary people, and how the most brazen of those scammers utilize society in their swindles, audaciously referring to laws that were supposed to defend good business, and wringing rules to turn against the victims with fraudulent language and point-blank threats. A smooth pickpocket can earn some respect for his swift ways of stealing without anyone getting hurt, but a cheat businessman who puts up a slick facade for the office and hires lawyers to involve the institutes of society that were supposed to protect the little man and the honest shopkeepers, indeed making the economic institutes of society partaking in the extortion and turn common resources against innocent people, is in my eyes the lowliest of economic criminals.

I like transparency because it is a much needed part of an immune defense against the deceitful bacteria circulating in the world of business. It also helps the good parts shine, by giving more light on them in increased visibility.

I really like well-managed, honest businesses that strive for low friction. They tend to show a sporty clarity while they deliver useful products with pride. To such corporations, I will gladly be a loyal customer, hopeful investor, engaged worker, friendly advocator.

My hope with this book is that it could give inspiration to good people working for well-intending, well-managed corporations, so that those businesses can become even greater: find and keep more customers, develop even better products, and retain a skillful and engaged workforce.

Transparency in commercial enterprise implies that people may discuss *most* matters, with anyone inside and outside the company, and have access to a historically unsurmounted amount of details about what is happening in, and around, the company. This is the good side of the coin, and I hope this trend will continue and grow even stronger in the future of business worldwide.

But the benevolent act to smoke out bad business via radically increased insight, must also be correctly counterbalanced with a respect for the privacy of regular people who are just doing their jobs. There must also be a good sense to let some internal, everyday teamwork solutions to everyday problems remain relatively private in order to maximize team efficiency and spirit, and obviously to also let invented techniques remain reasonably proprietary to an honest business corporation just long enough so it can harvest something from the sow before competitors sweep in.

There is indeed a conflict of interest gradually arising. Appropriate calibration of confidentiality is important to not *loose* trust. Over-sharing inflicts on privacy, and can touch the borders delimiting against industrial espionage.

Even for topics that fall well within such limits, there is insecurity within management that ongoing, multi-channel, multi-person communications are not and can not be controlled, and although controlling is not the intent, how can this whirlwind of communication streams become part of corporate strategy?

To begin answer this question, and regain a new comfort of joint direction, we will make a short odyssey through a few historical spotlights and touch some relevant management ideas, and from that form a simple, yet guiding metaphor for this whole problem set. Before we embark, let us first agree that all metaphors of organizations are paradoxical: the symbols provided can help us see more easily what is at hand, and can give guidance on what to do, but while doing exactly that, they also risk limiting our outlook, sometimes even obscure, since a metaphor is always a simplification.

A challenge for many of us in our modern professional lives, is to keep striving to become more and more skilled in the art of mobilizing metaphors just in time, so that we continuously find fresh ways of seeing and shaping situations[2]. New imagery can help us proceeding in this endeavor - and we should never give up challenging the cognitive traps we repeatedly put ourselves in.

The core proposition of this book comes as a simple metaphor of an open enterprise, a picture that is easy to remember. This is because I believe that simplicity in itself is crucial for a good metaphor, in order to be useful in strategic development work and for own

---

[2] As was wisely advised in Morgan (2006).

reflections. Overcomplicating a model may look impressive on a seminar, but does not help anyone in the field.

I am aware that most office workers in English-speaking countries associate the word "cube" with a cell in a drudging landscape office environment. In this book however, every mention of the word cube is for an idealistic abstraction of a corporate entity as a whole. It will display its axes of Resources, Operations, and Products, and its sides of Capacity, Allocation, and Delivery. The metaphoric material of glass is chosen because it is impelling when discussing transparency and its limits.

Organizational theory is a part of the social sciences of artificial worlds; places where predictions and self-fulfilling phenomena are impossible to separate from each other[3]. Glass Cube Strategy is to a high extent a concept, not a research finding: there is no particular group of companies that are using it in full already, while others not at all. Without anything even near a proper control group, it is not, and can not be, an academic theory (in the meaning that it would be built up from one or several unfalsifiable statements).

[3] See Bolman and Deal (1984), p.237

Rather, it is a proposed viewpoint, and a suggested tool for practitioners.

A metaphor for business strategy work, need to be simple enough to be quickly understandable, yet complex enough to admit many of the difficult topics that need resolution. It could also be expanded or altered or discarded depending on what discussion is at hand. Every metaphor is just an addition to all the thousand others that already are in use in our language, not a replacement to any one of them. A good metaphor can help discussions stay constructive while uncovering problems and finding solutions. Sometimes they are not needed, and then they are put aside.

It goes with the territory that an idea-oriented book is sent off with a trace of grue that some passage from its content can be twisted into an excuse to disturb some poor fellow who just went about working in peace when got hit in the head with some argumentative quote. Although that small risk exists, it is easily still worth the essay, considering how harmless most management books are in the real world (both for the literally hitting on heads, and as more sophisticated weapon of argumentation).

I wish that the metaphor of a Glass Cube can become an addition to the language of modern business, and as such, a help. I sincerely hope that the principles presented herein will be immediately usable in fine efforts in the field.

I will admit that I wrote the book for my own encouragement. The same wishes of encouragement go unabridged to the reader.

《》

Part I
BLACK AND GREY BLOBS

1

Towards Corporate Transparency

The suggestion of instilling more corporate transparency, amid heavy competition, and in the middle of
a million other daily struggles, may seem naïve, tiresome, even nonsensical.

But when looking back at the history of commercial development, the whole landscape of business is in
a long-term progression: away from black "blobs", and
towards networked arrays of much more transparent
entities that are interconnected in increasingly sophisticated ways.

This development within the commercial sector is
important also for the economy in society as a whole,
because additional voluntary disclosure decreases un-
derinvestments and therefore increases total wealth in

the economy, simply by improved economic efficiency without rising average cost of capital[4].

How stakeholders view the prospects for a firm, is always important for a business, not least during the start-up phase. Although transparency in general is good, there are a few exceptions. During the early life of a corporation, it is not necessarily a good thing to prematurely spend too much valuable time and resources on achieving the level of information quality and elaborate track records needed to respond to full scrutiny from public investors. Too much transparency too soon can be costly when making innovative and non-contractible investments, if uncontrolled spill-over gains are transferred to some early stakeholders. In those situations, it is rational to commence on a slightly less transparent ambition: not hand out all platform details to all early customers, and not target the broad investor community, only taking private placements, while information quality on the firm's quality increases[5]. But the business idea, the product basics, and an overview of operational resources should be no secrets, even for a most risky start-up.

---

[4] Cheynel (2013).

[5] Almazan et.al. (2007).

I will use the term "black blob" for a business that is not freely disclosing to anyone that asks, what it is essentially about, how it operates, and with what resources. Secrecy on such fundamental matters, darkness even, is unquestionably intentional. The shady firms that are most difficult to reach and understand, are often purposedly so, typically because they are built on dishonest foundations. Most corporations are not so opaque, but those "black blobs" tend to get into trouble eventually, while its background shadows escape like soundless serpents to their next dark operation. These opaque scamsters cause a lot of accumulated grief and frustration in society, year after year; countermeasures against them need to be improved, locally, nationally, and globally.

The difficulty with the extreme cases, when the organization owes its main sustenance to some seclusion from insight, is that the great deceivers employ all of the typical substances of apparent openness and with theatrical mastery feign honesty about their mission; those scams often have unusually beautiful facades, but just "forgets" to mention one or two paramount facts. The black blob is there, in the very core of the corporate existence, but then there is so much pomp and circumstance around it, that the whole spectacle can be mistaken for an honest endeavor.

«»

I would suggest that the vast majority of organizations today are something of "grey blobs", i.e., they disclose many facts and particular status reports about their operations, based on what they must report due to regulatory demands and external pressures from stakeholders and customers, and this is complemented with sporadic extras, but, apart from that, not too much spare effort is spent on clearly presenting other relevant data on ongoing relevant and vital matters in an easily retrievable and directly understood form.

In addition, they typically have marketing functions or a secretary that try to control exactly what messages are supposed to be spread publicly, and when. Long traditions of defensive closure means there there also is a fundamental uneasiness in a grey blob about the sharing of facts, and there are both formal policies or informal understandings in place to control external communications, hoping that isolation of management processes makes life so much easier and that quietness will not cause any unnecessary questions.

«»

In their daily operation, normal grey blobs can't avoid frustrating customers and their own employees, by never giving the whole picture on anything, by causing wobbling indecision, and generally half-cut measures. Most of the time, active censorship is not needed, because the information sharing channels are just not efficient anyway, and there is no real willingness to communicate rapidly and openly to all stakeholders. Customer communications may be contradictory, weak, and disincentivized, leading to only sporadic and unsystematic insights into current overall status or into upcoming events that should be of interest.

I suppose working in a grey blob can feel like being a relatively skilled oarsman in a Roman or ancient Greek navy galley ship. No, I don't mean to imply slavery at all. Contrary to common conception today, those ancient navy oarsmen were only in exceptional cases slaves or prisoners of war. Mostly, they were maritime employees[6]. As paid labor, they were trained for the task but, apart from that, supposed to sit down, listen to the drumbeat, and keep rowing. Everyone onboard a galley must realize that the whole ship would stop moving if all oarsmen dropped their oars to discuss seating arrangements, or quietly ponder the philosophical nature of the oncoming waves. So, and this is the similarity of grinding in a grey blob, the focus is to keep rowing - without caring where the ship is going or knowing what the navy is up to, really.

To take that analogy a little bit further, the trouble with the old naval infantry, was that circumstances did not always let the ship move straight ahead in a steady pace in fairly calm weather, which was the surroundings a galley was best suited to. The ocean had an annoying habit of tossing a galley around and throwing the completely wrong winds at it. Between sporadic moments of storm-ridden drama, the days and nights on a galley must have been filled with boredom and horrible pain from repetitive movements while rowing. The galley was not an agile vehicle, but could move

---

[6] According to written sources, rowing was recognized as an honorable profession, perfectly acceptable to any freeman who wished to earn some money. Hence, a typical contract assignment or even like a regular employment. See Sargent(1927).

ahead, as long as circumstances allowed. Not too different from how most mature businesses strides along in their enterprise environment.

«»

Another problem with the boredom of working in a grey blob, is that it reinforces itself into more permanent disillusion. Is it not saddening that the overwhelming majority of adults in the industrialized countries get more thrill from watching tv in the evening in the sofa at home, than during their long hours of work? Even though what happens at work is for real, affecting real people, as opposed to the tv drama.

Instead of work being something of an adventure, it is, as we all know, often repetitious and (more or less) humiliating. Granted, being self-employed or running a small business can replace some of the boredom with a little more anxiety instead, but no matter which type of contract, paid work - being work - can typically only replace some tiring or humiliating factors with some others. Therefore, salaries to compensate. In the end, most people settle for a regular employment that is reasonably tiresome and reasonably well-paid, and seek the comfort of having some sense of foresight regarding their private finances, in some cases even an illusion of financial safety until retirement and beyond (even if the true horizon of one's job income is in reality often only a few months away at best, and a couple of management decisions in between). In this self-delusion of financial safety, comes also an acceptance that management hierarchy is effective and that foot soldiers, as a mere minimum, shall pretend that the pep talks given, actually have effect and increase motivation. The leaders, looking down on the whining cadres, forget that it is thanks to the control structures that any work is being done at all; so when people don't feel in control or have insight into the bigger events, it is merely human to resort to complaining about irrelevant details and overly obsess over trivial questions; where is the fruit basket, and who took the bananas.

When an employee is spending all day inside a grey blob with limited visibility, many contradictory things tend to happen, especially in the relations in line hierarchy: a manager that (with best intent) shares information about the near future can get abysmally entangled in followup questions and adjacent discussions. In the worst case derailed for some time, and more stressed for time compared with the manager that shares less with the team, following the good old "need-to-know" mentality, or compared with those who play helpless to avoid expectations from their subordinates, and of course also even more so compared with the fugitive managers that are practically unreachable.

If it is demoralizing for employees to try interact in a grey blob, the same goes for customers that hang at the perimeters. For a customer interacting with a grey blob, it can be like trying to throw a tennis ball towards a fairly small hole in a large wall of concrete. If you don't aim properly, the ball will either bounce back to you, or quietly drop to the ground. This concrete wall was built to protect the laborers behind the wall, who are probably busy doing something (but you don't know what). For a customer though, the whole experience of receiving bouncing balls (or giving up on all the never-returning ones), is nothing but utterly disappointing.

As will be explored in later chapters, there are ways to systematically prepare and simplify communication flows, encourage minimizing of greyness, order work to trim down the concrete walls, and - through using a crispier vocabulary - help to better orchestrate the many voices that are sounded, maybe even into one symphony.

But first, let's go even further into darkness. I promise it will be so dark that it will be amusing.

2

An Undertaking of Great Advantage

A centerpiece of a corporate entity is that it can survive longer than a physical person, and potentially muster more resources over its lifespan than its individual shareholders could separately. As opposed to a human, a moderately well-run corporation can, in theory, exist in perpetuity as a going concern.

However, the potential longevity is not the main attraction of the corporate entity idea. The huge success of joint-stock companies in the world economy is thanks to the limited liabilities concept, creating the separate legal personality of the corporation. The corporation as a legal person liable for its economic undertakings, can over time start showing something like a personality in its actions[7] and expectations. As a side

---

[7] Those not too positive about modern capitalism enjoy to point out that two of the first really big companies, the Dutch and the English East India, had similar modus operandi as conquistadors.

effect, this "persona" issue of a corporation has also proven to be an area for great delusions.

From the dawn of time, humans have practiced to judge quickly whether to trust another human we meet, or not. Sometimes we are right, sometimes wrong. In any case, there has not been anything in our biological past to prepare us for relating to abstract, legal entities. Although the perceived trustworthiness of people involved in the corporation can sometimes be a proxy for how much we can believe in the corporation, it is not enough. We must also include facts about the corporation itself into the decision base. This is hard. Some facts are always concealed, be it with people or corporations.

Clever people who funnel their creativity and industriousness into challenging ventures, is at the heart of the bloodstream of the modern market economy.

Unfortunately, cunning people playing similar tones are tapping that very same bloodstream, like vampires from their victims. To add to the drama, a person can go from clever to cunning in a month, if fear and greed take hold, and a corporation can be mostly good one year and bad the next. The history of capitalism is filled of shooting stars turning into disgraceful rubble practically overnight.

To run or understand commercial ventures, whether new or old, or to manage equity investments in them, we must first acknowledge the look and feel of the hostile forces of deception in the world of enterprise. A good source for this orientation is to read damage reports from speculation and fraud, for the very same reasons that medical staff need to study autopsy protocols, and vehicle designers need to read accident reports.

Let us pick one short report. There are thousands of stories in the history of business, but this one amuses me most in its simplicity.

In 1852, Charles Mackay wrote a splendid book about delusional investment schemes; setups where greed won over rationality (as long as share prices kept rising). Many such schemes stirred up in the wake of the South-Sea Company[8],, sparkling like bubbles in a glass of champagne, and created so much disarray that they provoked a law in Britain called the Bubble Act[9].

---

[8] The dazzling inspiration for this venture was of course the British East India Company (1600-1874).

[9] The South-Sea Company started in 1711 and in 1719 had such inflated value that it took on to repay most the public debt of

The following is but one of all those creative proposals, the most creative one. Mackay describes how in overall delusion, many people believed that if only they were quick enough to react on news, and get in early in new ventures, they could make a lot of money out of thin air.

One memorable passage from Mackay's book[10], is this description of an event in 1720 about a venture with an unforgettable investment pitch:

> In the mean time, innumerable joint-stock companies started up every where. They soon received the name of Bubbles, the most appropriate that imagination could devise. The populace are often most happy in the nicknames they employ. None could be more apt than that of Bubbles. Some of them lasted for a week or a fortnight, and were no more heard

England (via a trade monopoly offered by the crown). This setup was received so advantageous that the stock ballooned in value, with a speculating frenzy that inspired hundreds of completely unrelated other projects, more or less realistic. New share issues in all kinds of ideas were quickly subscribed for in a frantic pace in Change Alley of London (the stock market of those days). Brokers were as busy then as ever: sometimes the current quotes differed between different parts of the alley in rapid trading, that fuelled the craze even more.

[10] Mackay (1852), p.54.

of, while others could not even live out that short span of existence. Every evening produced new schemes, and every morning new projects.

But the most absurd and preposterous of all, and which shewed, more completely than any other, the utter madness of the people, was one started by an unknown adventurer, entitled

"A company for carrying on an undertaking of great advantage, but nobody to know what it is."

Were not the fact stated by scores of credible witnesses, it would be impossible to believe that any person could have been duped by such a project. The man of genius who essayed this bold and successful inroad upon public credulity, merely stated in his prospectus that the required capital was half a million, in five thousand shares of 100£. each, deposit 2£ per share. Each subscriber, paying his deposit, would be entitled to 100£ per annum per share. How this immense profit was to be obtained, he did not condescend to inform them at that time, but promised that in a month full particulars should be duly announced, and a call made for the remaining 98£ of the subscription.

Next morning, at nine o'clock, this great man opened an office in Cornhill. Crowds of people beset his door, and when he shut up at three o'clock, he found that no less than one thousand shares had been subscribed for, and the deposits paid.

He was thus, in five hours, the winner of 2000£. He was philosopher enough to be contented[11] with his venture, and set off the same evening for the Continent. He was never heard of again.

There it is. This eternally refreshing lesson from 1720 screams to us that when a business model involves enormous secrecy, something is probably very, very wrong.

---

[11] According to a calculation on MeasuringWorth.com in December 2014, that monetary amount in 1720 can be compared against historic measurements for contemporary standard of living in the London area, and found to be equal to the effect of receiving 261,000 £ in today. However, if comparing that sum for its "economic power value" in society (relating it to the national GDP), it could be like receiving 29,000,000 £ in cash today. Yes, twenty-nine million pounds, for just one day of "work"! Bon voyage!

«»

The essence of openness in the world of business, is not that transparency itself lines out in advance exactly *what* all enterprises should do, or details *how* they should do it.

Instead, it provides one distinct rule; to dare always have a frank dialogue with all stakeholders, and honestly display as much as possible about what is happening in and around the enterprise at each moment, good or bad. We will return to practical recommendations on that in Part III.

The courage to arrange and encourage transparency rises from basically trusting that, as a consequence to openness, if the purpose is basically good, and common interest in this purpose remains, benevolent assistance will join forces, and good things will materialize.

To execute strategic transparency in a corporation is to voluntarily mount many spotlights, so that no corner is unlit or murky. The corporation will be thriving in the clear, completely visible, as the undertaking will

be presented openly. Everybody should know what it
is.

3

Various Spotlights
(1712-2012)

Now, let's start to put some light into the darkness!
Well, not bright sunlight exactly, more similar to a few
spotlights, that glow and add some circles of
brightness in an otherwise mostly murky locale.

First, we will discuss the centuries-long progress
from viewing knowledge-sharing as industrial espionage or treason, towards more openness between
competing firms, around technology matters and various best practices. Secondly, we will look into the
books of accounting and how the gradually opened financial records can be seen as more spotlights being
installed, one by one, voluntarily or not.

Industrial Espionage in 1712

Like countries in conflict needing to defend their military technology, companies have always seen valid reason to protect their valuable intellectual property from dishonest competitors. Good competitors play according to the rules (i.e., license technology, or try find new ideas of their own), whereas bad competitors are willing to break contracts, or steal another company's trade secrets, to get ahead.

To create wealth and prosperity, states and corporations have long worked together to create well-functioning markets, where good, hard work should win over criminal or immoral methods. The intent is simply that investment should be encouraged, but not stealing.

Over time, industries have seen the institutionalization of many secrecy concerns, into intellectual property laws, entrance barriers, employee laws, and standard terms in contracts. Sometimes these rules are respected completely, sometimes not. In any case, a great deal of energy is spent to either defend or acquire or circumvent various competitive assets.

Curiosity, willingness to take initiative, and inventiveness, are all virtues in enterprise. With the creative destruction that is inherent in capitalism, comes the fear of not knowing what is around, so observing attentively is a natural response. What is vigilant observation and what is immoral espionage is not always totally easy to define.

A letter 1712 to Paris from a Jesuit father stationed in China, revealed the manufacturing methods for hardened porcelain, and this communication is sometimes considered an early case of industrial espionage.

Manufacturers in Europe took advantage of learning these techniques, and the export volumes of porcelain from China then began to shrink dramatically[12]. In retrospect, the case is much milder considering that a couple of Germans had independently discovered how to produce hardened porcelain already in 1707 and even established a factory for that in Meissen 1710; at least two years before any copies of that letter from China was beginning to circulate[13]. In other words, competitive intelligence[14] could probably have helped factories in Europe improve their production tech-

---

[12] As retold in *China's Last Empire: The Great Qing* from 2009 by William T. Rowe (p.84).

[13] See under porcelain in The Columbia Encyclopedia, 6th ed.

niques soon enough, with or without that famous letter.

The matters of competitive secrecy in industry with ever larger sums of money at stake, has definitely not disappeared from business life since the porcelain affairs of 1712. Today, there are concerns voiced by journalists and nonprofit activists that experienced ex-military officers and ex-police officers are employed by corporations as security and intelligence staff, and there continue to use methods learned as government employees, networking with ex-colleagues, even contracting special service suppliers to do unsavory operations[15]. The allegation is that those operations include surveillance, infiltration, and disruption of watchdogs such as non-governmental organizations, should they be perceived as threats to the corporate brand and reputation.

---

[14] As opposed to industrial espionage, competitive intelligence is an ethical and legal business activity. Part of business intelligence, this function in a company is responsible for early identification of risks and opportunities in the market before they become obvious, and is supposed to be especially looking for early signals of new entrants besides the current main competitors, in particular if the new entrant seems to be using new models for production or pricing, or utilizing new technology.

[15] Alleged in article by Jeremy Scahill, "Blackwater's Black Ops" October 4, 2010. The Nation magazine.

During the Cold War, industrial espionage was a serious issue, and the methods continue to this day, and seek new targets. For companies in military industrial segments, espionage is a constant headache, for obvious reasons. But secrecy also became an integrated part of how professional behavior was defined in most industries around the world.

The question to consider now, in ordinary companies, is to what extent fierce guarding of relatively mundane information as trade secrets, or worrying about disclosure of market plans by ex-employees, or sweeping concerns about the financial status under the carpet, or engaging in clandestine confrontation with nonprofit associations to avoid their attention, are constructive parts of a long-term rational business behavior.

Instead, I would argue that self-confident openness builds trust that can turn into a surprising strength when facing investors, customers, and employees. In this book, we therefore explore the possibilities of openness as a strategic choice.

The intent is of course not to instigating anyone to gossip in the name of sharing, to breach any contract, behave reckless or untrustworthy, or in any way promote acts of industrial espionage. Leaking sensitive information can be devastating for business relations that are built on trust, and if taken to the level of contract breach, might be liable or even criminal.

The discussion that follows on corporate transparency, is meant to inspire policy-level strategic management choices and contemplated cultural shifts. Not to applaud any individual trickery or to generally defend any unprofessional misjudgments in communications that have occurred or will occur.

Just to conclude our very brief comparison between business and warfare, note how the tone expressed in some competitive moments of business operations continue to be similar to that of sports, or even warfare; stirring the same fear that the arch-enemy will get the upper hand if we don't stay on our toes, and that winning means glorious victory over the enemy. Because of their long-run popularity, all these comparisons with combat or sports can become tiresome. Although sometimes well versed quotes, there is a numbness creeping in after some amount of rehashing words from long-dead Chinese generals or aged football coaches. Not all employees feel the same about such competitive pep talk, but all are expected to nod and cheer to the pep. Times are changing, though. Very soon, it will not be particularly cool for a business executive anywhere in the world to try sound like an army major shouting troops into battle. In the future, such speech will still be made for humor, with a twinkle in the eye. Although the competitive element remains, the future-proof business has another level of respect for its skilled staff, and presents a more relevant view on what constitutes bravery in the workplace.

Internal Accounts in 1926

The next spotlight takes us to accounting. Yes, in the sporadically dramatic history of financial reporting, it was a sensational moment when the chairman of the conglomerate Lever Brothers[16] in 1926 disclosed the firm's total consolidated sales numbers for the previous year. The general public was allowed to know the turnover in pounds sterling of the big conglomerate; this was far from a standard insight at the time:

---

[16] Transformed into Unilever in 1937.

> "On the whole, the directors [of Lever Brothers] are to be commended for their continued efforts to introduce greater clarity into the company's accounts. We would urge them not to be weary in well-doing, but to take an even bolder step next year, and publish a combined balance sheet incorporating the accounts of the subsidiary companies".

> The Economist, 7 April 1928.

Then from 1927 to 1931, the chairman of Lever, Mr. Cooper, even disclosed their profit by product lines and by regions. In retrospect presenting a break-down like that is more exciting to see than whatever the figures were. Press clips on these events show a mix of feelings over this voluntary openness about corporate bookkeeping. In one article in 1929, the Economist praised Lever Brothers, but went on to warn its readers about trying to analyze a consolidated balance sheet: "it is unwise to hazard an interpretation of movements in these enormous items"[17].

In the USA, it was not until the end of the 1960s that a first *recommendation* to report profit per busi-

---

[17] This description of Unilever's history is from Camfferman, K. and Zeff, S.A. (2003). p.177.

ness segment was issued by the Accounting Principles Board. During the preceding years, several conglomerates had been created, some spanning multiple countries, making them hard to analyze. However, these multi-national corporations objected to having to disclose revenues and profits per segments, to avoid "tipping off" competitors on which geography or product line was more profitable than another. Lobbying prevented any further attempt at the time to make segment reporting mandatory. In the end, the board could only issue an opinion of recommendation[18].

More Mandatory Reporting in 2008

Fast forward to the third spotlight: In the aftermath of the 2008 financial crisis, better insight of financial risk exposures of financial institutions became an international regulatory objective, not least from the commitments from the "G-20 Washington Summit on Financial Markets and the World Economy" meeting held in 2008.

---

[18] This history of the development of generally accepted accounting principles and political pressures was exposed in Nobes and Parker (2008). p.215.

As a consequence, supervisory authorities now receive an enormous amount of data on the type of financial derivatives contracts that were at the center of the turmoil of 2008. Whether all that data is analyzed into meaningful statistics is another question, but that it had to be assembled, forced improvements of internal administration and controlling within the reporting institutes. Granted, there will be more credit crises ahead, but the importance was the interruption of practically giving complete *laissez-faire* for banks in regards to their credit exposures, combined with unspoken government guarantees to bail out big firms when they got in trouble. The main alternatives painfully brought to the table was that either banks could remain   in their freedom of partial darkness, *or* they needed be regulated more, monitored more closely than before, and forced to disclose more of their ongoing business. The latter case meant loosing some freedom, and adding more work and costs into the reporting processes, but also gaining some forced self-help action to steer more clear from the worst bankruptcy dangers. In 2008, politicians in G20 were faced with those two alternatives, and chose to turn on the spotlight. Other problems will arise, like always in the history of finance, but the overall trend is towards less opaque banking.

Open-Book Accounting in 2012

To conclude this short series of spotlights, we will touch the term "open-book accounting", which refers to a systematic and voluntary disclosure of economic information between cooperating entities, information that traditionally was kept only within corporate borders.

The initial emphasis of this concept has been concerned with joint cost reductions in long-term collaborative relationships, by improving insight into supply chains and applying inter-organizational cost management techniques.[19]

Traditionally, open-book accounting has mostly been used between partners in "dyadic" relationships, with specific information exchanged at agreed times for a specific purpose[20], in selected links in a supply chain. In my opinion, this partially formalized setup

---

[19] Described in Das (2011).

[20] See Hoffjan, Lührs, and Kolburg (2011).

around a supply chain cooperation, is a light version of a consortium.

Examples of supply cooperation are drawn from manufacturing industries, but another good illustration of a for-profit special-purpose consortium is when a group of banks collaborate to make a syndicated loan. The bank syndication is then a light consortium, and the partners rightfully require of each other that there be open books on the syndicated loan conditions and its performance.

Organizations funded by charity or with government funding for societal or charitable purposes will also increasingly have to use open-book accounting as part of their normal setup, to comply with tighter anti-corruption policies from the funding partners, and to meet increased expectations of goal followup, and efficiency metrics.

The International Aid Transparency Initiative (IATI) was launched in 2008 to meet political commitments on transparency in aid, development, and humanitarian resources. As of October 2015, there were submissions from 352 organizations into the IATI database[21]. Looking at publishing statistics according to

---

[21] See www.iatiregistry.org for more information.

IATI's own assessment scoring at that time, the highest score for statistics comprehensiveness was given to Gavi the Vaccine Alliance, which is a public-private global health partnership committed to immunization in poor countries. I hope that initiatives like this will help global development work to focus on what is effective.

An inspiring moment for voluntary open-books accounting came in 2012 when the Park Theatre was about to open in Finsbury Park in London[22] (hence the title of this spotlight section being 2012): The artistic director insisted that all producers renting the premises should use open-book accounting.

This would allow cast, creatives and crew in a production to see financial data on their show. Apparently, there had been problems in London theaters with opaque "profit-share" contracts, where participants just have had to accept a message afterwards that there were no profits, no matter if a show ran with full audience or not.

One actor was hopeful that this new openness from producers on financial details, can lead to less disappointments over payments:

---

[22] Gardner (2012)

"The reason we moan is because we feel disempow-
ered. People don't want to speak out because they
are afraid of getting a reputation as a troublemaker.
Open-book accounting is just a way of informing everyone on the show how and where the money is
being spent. To me, it just makes sense. You may still
end up working for free, but at least you know why
you are exploiting yourself."

Actor Rebecca Peyton, quoted in The Guardian[23]

In the future, it will simply not be possible to expect
anyone to feel a shared intention, about a business, or
charity, or cultural production, without getting ample
insight in where the money actually went.

---

[23] Gardner (2012)

4

The Huge Grey Blob

If an unscrupulous venture fraud such as "an Undertaking of Great Advantage" mentioned previously, is a small black blob, then world society today is *the* huge grey blob (with a few bright spots here and there).

This is a book on corporate transparency, so I will not go too far into the huge grey blob, and risk getting lost. But there are some overlapping concepts, and definitely lessons to be learned from societal policies, so let us now just take a quick look on transparency policies in society at large.

Transparency Policies in Society

The concept of transparency is really fundamental in a democratic society in general, and also of rising urgency for solving contemporary global issues that know no national borders.

In four areas, I would suggest that highly effective transparency policies are of extra importance for the future of humanity, and the progress of society: Planetary Survival, Public Safety, Political System Cleanliness, and Economy Cleanliness.

In each of these areas, there are particular domains that looks particularly critical. Here is an attempt to list on a very general level, these most important areas:

1   Planetary Survival

    1.1   Biosphere Impact

        1.1.1   Pollution control

        1.1.2   Deforestation control

    1.2   Environment Monitoring

2   Public Safety

    2.1   Violent Crime, Terrorism, and War

    2.2   Infectious Diseases

    2.3   Drinking Water and Food Safety

    2.4   Medical Safety

    2.5   Workplace Safety

    2.6   Product Safety

3   Political Cleanliness

    3.1   Anti-Corruption

For the future of all humanity, implementing and reinforcing the society transparency policies listed above, are of paramount importance, for all of us. Researchers are busy studying how different policies for transparency have been implemented in these areas and themes, and how influential the policies have been so far.[24]

Although the scope and the stakeholders differ - and of course the severity of impact when there are

---

[24] In their 2008 study, authors Fung, Graham, and Wheel, indicated that in the USA, corporate financial disclosure (part of point 4.1 above) had been more effective than nutritional labeling (part of point 2.3) and toxic release disclosure (part of point 1.1.1). This did not mean that everything about financial reporting was fine (showcased by the fact that concurrent with their study being published, there was a big credit crisis arising). But it is worth noting that effects of information flows can be surprisingly different: investors (as a community) seemed to pay more immediate attention if a company was derailing or was hiding something important about its books, compared with consumers

failures in execution – general sharing of experiences can be made between policies in the mentioned areas for society, and implementing the Glass Cube Strategy for a corporation.

Anti-Corruption

I listed "anti-corruption" under "political cleanliness" because corruption tend to get most ugly when taxes (supposedly and forcedly paid for the common good) is redirected and stolen, or purloined to various bribes, or when public officials are accepting bribes to make non-objective decisions to favor the bribing source, simultaneously undermining the value and respect of political office.

The worst cases are called "Grand Corruption"; those cases can even involve national legislation, law-enforcement, etc., giving the corrupt person in power an explicit or practical immunity to continue the thieving.

Unfortunately, money-laundering facilities and front nominees are still churning criminal money to an

---

not getting proper information on their food items, or even risks of poisoning.

enormous extent, as indicated in released data from whistle-blowers now and then.

So far, I have not heard of any good reason why the "beneficial owner" of assets anywhere would be allowed to be kept secret from tax authorities and police investigators, by any bank, commercial depository, or official ownership registry.

Obviously, anti-corruption policies are also very important in the "Anti-Fraud" work within the commercial sector (i.e. part of "Economic Cleanliness" in the tabulation above). For example, a manager with any influence on a procurement decisions, or a consultant hired to analyze procurement alternatives and give impartial advice, can not receive payment[25] from a vendor in exchange for selection or recommendation; all trust shown by the employer or client for that bribed individual is then spoiled.

Multinational corporations have the extra challenge in their organizations, to not fall into local traps, and not to become implicated in overseas bribery scan-

---

[25] This type of bribery payment comes under many different names: "kick-back", "success fee", "sales commission", are the most commonly heard of at the moment. Anything more than entertaining a normal lunch during a break in scheduled presentations, is pushing the limit.

dals. Wherever there is a corrupted political class, we can not put hopes upon regulatory sanctions or criminal prosecution. Due to historical traditions, and the lack of effective local implementation of international conventions, there are obviously still many practical limitations of transnational criminal sanctioning by sovereign actors for fully countering international bribery[26].

Voluntary transparency that will open up for an early and compelling market-force sanctioning of attempts of embezzlement, together with an increased global self-regulation of the majority of legitimate business that are all working on the honest side of the line, must instead be used in a more wide-spread way as part of a hybrid response mechanisms to counter national and transnational corruption. When fear of punishment is not enough, removing opportunities can work better.

---

[26] See Lord (2014) for detailed discussion on responses to transnational corporate bribery.

Privacy

Of course, innocent people must not suffer from well-meaning Anti-Corruption work, e.g. overly disrupting their lives without cause. Balancing with privacy aspects is therefore used as a counterweight in the transparency work.

The "nothing to hide" argument is prevalent in popular debates pressing for full disclosures on every data at all times. However, that argument is too simplistic.

First, some data may feed the criminals more than the law enforcers, if published online without prior consideration. Second, for a corporation as such, the concept of privacy does not apply directly (instead there are contractual confidentiality clauses and espionage acts to adhere to). But employees and customers are individuals, and a correct privacy level for them is to be respected in a civilized society. Therefore, as the corporation increases its transparency, there must be safeguards for employee and customer privacy. This sounds easy, but what, then, is privacy?

Daniel J. Solove at George Washington University Law School argued[27] that we should approach privacy as a set of parallel resemblances[28], not defined as a singular essence, but a plurality of related concepts. Solove points out that privacy policy solutions thus far have been focusing too much on the Orwell metaphor (government surveillance and social control), and not adequately addressing the Kafka problems (information processing effects).

The Kafka problems gradually affect power relationships between people and their institutions (including employers, suppliers, and other corporations), by not only frustrating the individual by creating a sense of helplessness, but also indirectly affect social structures by altering the types of relationships people have with institutions that make various decisions about their lives[29]:

---

[27] Solove, D.J. (2007).

[28] That some concepts do not have one thing in common but are related to one another in many different ways. In the words of Wittgenstein (1953); instead of being related by a common denominator, some things share "a complicated network of similarities overlapping and crisscrossing: sometimes overall similarities, sometimes similarities of detail."

[29] Kafka,F. (1935).

"So, then I'll be free," said K. doubtfully. "That's right," said the painter, "but only apparently free or, to put it a better way, provisionally free, as the most junior judges, the ones I know, they don't have the right to give the final acquittal. Only the highest court can do that, inaccessible to you, to me and for all of us. We don't know prospects there and, incidentally, we don't want to know. The right to acquit people is a major privilege and our judges don't have it, but they do have the right to free people from the indictment. That's to say, if they're freed in this way then for the time being the charge is withdrawn but it's still hanging over their heads and it only takes an order from higher up to bring it back into force.

And as I'm in such good contact with the court I can also tell you how the difference between absolute and apparent acquittal is described, just in a superficial way, in the directives to the court offices. If there's an absolute acquittal documents disappears from the process, not just the charge but the trial and even the acquittal disappears, everything is destroyed.

With an apparent acquittal it's different. The documents remain, except that the case for your acquittal was added. Apart from that, the dossier go on as before, the case gets passed to higher courts, back down to the lower courts and so on, oscillates backwards and forwards, sometimes faster, sometimes slower. It's impossible to calculate exactly what's happening.

From outside it can sometimes seem that everything has been forgotten, documents been lost and the acquittal is complete. No-one familiar with the court would believe that. No documents ever get lost, the court forgets nothing.

One day, unexpectedly, some judge or other picks up the documents and looks at them, notices that the charge is still valid, and orders the defendant's immediate arrest. I've been talking here as if there's a long delay between apparent acquittal and re-arrest, that is quite possible and I do know of cases like that, but it's just as likely that the defendant goes home after he's been acquitted and finds police there already waiting to re-arrest him.

The quote from Kafka's novel illustrates how a privacy problem occurs when information handling by an individual, business, or government entity creates undue harm by disrupting the life of a person. To prepare for designing safeguards against having the corporation, in a benevolent effort of transparency, causing harm by privacy oversteps, we will now explore this topic one step deeper.

As a way of mapping the harms that constitute privacy violations, and after studying the welter of laws, cases, issues, and cultural and historical materials, Solove developed a taxonomy of privacy. He listed four general categories and with a total of sixteen subcategories of privacy challenges and problems:

Category 1: Information Collection

Surveillance

Interrogation

Category 2: Information Processing

Aggregation

Identification

Insecurity[30]

Secondary Use

Exclusion[31]

---

[30] Increasing a person's vulnerability to potential abuse of their personal information

[31] Inability to access and have a say in the way one's data is used.

Category 3: Information Dissemination

Breach of Confidentiality

Disclosure

Exposure

Increased Accessibility

Blackmail

Appropriation

Distortion

Category 4: Invasion

Intrusion

Decisional Interference

We will return to these hazards in Part III, and discuss appropriate safeguards as a part of practical work on resource transparency implementation. As related to policy on societal level, I must stress that the argumentation that while legal persons normally should "have nothing to hide", and thus have no serious issue with sharing relevant information about the business, this does not include unnecessarily displaying client data or employees whereabouts.

Managers in a corporation should lead by example and be very careful to not cause collegial pressure for public statements or online publishing on intranet or internet sites, of such comments that happen to be politically correct within that organization at that time, and other opinions about non-work related matters. The same applies for coerced circulation of photos of activities outside the workplace; what the staffer did with friends and family on vacation, and so forth. For all normal jobs, it is sufficient to come in and do a good job, without pressure to fraternize after work, involving family and friends, if such gatherings are not genuinely voluntary. It easily happens that integrity is not an appreciated collegial trait, but misunderstood for snobbery or haughty disinterest. Man is a social animal, and we are sensitive for group inclusion and of small signals of possible disinterest on either part. A culture of high integrity will encourage that cards be put on the table as soon as possible: what is expected, what is not necessary, and what is inadvisable. So, if the corporate persona is to be expected to show integrity in all its external relations, it must start internally with observing the manifested interpersonal culture between colleagues, as well as the genuine internal attitude with clients, in practice, daily.

In exceptional cases, such as for politicians, the private life, circle of friends, and the values displayed by a person seeking office, can be factors htat affect the voter's confidence, and in those situations, a reasonable openness with the constituency is expected, else journalistic investigations can be relevant. Being an employee at a corporation, a police officer, or an intern at a government office, is obviously quite different from running for Prime Minister when it comes to reasonable public attention to personal life. Therefore the level of disclosure that can be expected, should be very, very different. Although I argue that all corporations should strive to improve transparency towards its stakeholders in most matters, that shall not turn into vulgarizing form of coerced staff exhibits on social networks, trivial as they may be in the outset. Tastefulness, relevance, and tact are therefore indispensable filters for all postings online done in any *ex officio* capacity.

During the last decades, there is a troublesome trend of desensitization of the permanent nature of defaming records, like if persistently lingering past events and comments, true or not, is an unavoidable part of all modern life, making old jokes stick forever or fictions made up by others blurring reality perceptions of a person forever, maybe even slowly turning the epidemic of online ridicule into "a culture of humiliation" as in the words of Nicolaus Mills at the Sarah Lawrence College in New York.[32] Millions of online posts and re-posts are cascading "to the enterprise of immediately spreading embarrassing moments, or of exaggerating people's foibles".

This is the loss-of-privacy tempest wherein a sound corporate transparency strategy needs to navigate very carefully.

---

[32] Zaslow (2010).

5

Pressing for Corporate Transparency

As the role-reversals of consumption and production continues in many sectors, activist consumers as "brand ambassadors" keep on top of many media channels and voice concerns and beliefs, both on factual issues involving the brand, and on fictitious events or fabricated marketing material.

The pressure for increased transparency is not so much arising from external initiatives from journalists, as from a semi-internal expectation from loyal customers, together an internal expectation from employees who want to stay proud of their employer.

Voluntary disclosure items can come in the form of public replies or posts about day-to-day issues in the customer services department, often with a common, friendly, everyday tone. Trivial as some of the replies may seem from a trained marketing professional's eye, as they are typically lacking the refinement of copywriting, the human aspect of such comments can still help the brand, since they are putting humans up front. Another advantage with keeping up to speed in a dialogue is to not let online critique stand unanswered.

> "Let all your employees blab and blog. In the new world of radical transparency, the path to business success is clear".

> Clive Thompson in "The See-Through CEO"[33]

A majority of people probably realize that some noise from sporadic influx of disparate complaints is expected in a large commercial operation, and are not discouraged by these comments online. Only if the online critique looks more systematic it is reasonably suspected to be due to widespread problems, or if a complaint is extraordinarily well expressed or shocking, the post is spread very widely, crossing into high-

---

[33] Thompson (2007).

networked nodes like major news sites, and it will start really damage the reputation.

Interestingly, it is not a good general defense against online critique to try to stay out of online presence altogether, no matter if this inattention is because of ignorance, lack of engagement, or fear of the uncontrolled medium. Even a healthy corporation with happy customers, needs to be aware of its online persona, also when everything is fine and there are few mentions. If a bad comment appears and is for a considerable time the only, or one out of few lingering top comments, it has a relatively strong impact. For this reason, it is statistically better to allow many voices to speak:

> One bad blog post can kill you. But if you've got hundreds or thousands of sites linking to you and commenting on you, the law of averages takes over, and odds are the opinion will be accurate: The cranks will be outweighed by cooler heads. Again, the Net rewards the transparent.
>
> Peter Hirshberg in "The See-Through CEO"[34]

---

[34] Thompson (2007).

Now, we must not for a single moment be naïve about what can occur when encouraging employees to talk for and about their employer online. Of course, some serious and very damaging leaks can be triggered by a person's need for revenge, or if it is sensation-seeking rather than genuine concern of public interest. That also happened also in the old landscape of traditional printed media, but since the speed and reach is higher online than offline, minor conversations escalate quicker.

The overall conclusion is nevertheless, that an ongoing, healthy attention for a corporation's existence, is better than a complete disinterest in its business.

Also in product development, recruitment activities and other functions, an increased openness on current challenges and upcoming ambitions can act as a powerful tool to attract suppliers and employees.

《》

One consolation when fearing the loss of information advantages against competitors, can be the fact that innovation processes are path-dependent, i.e., built on recent successes, gives a momentum for further breakthroughs. So the leader can afford some degree of openness with its new product launches without too much worry. Because while the launch is taking place, the firm is already researching and developing the next upcoming offering.

Not only is the product development momentum a tough act to follow and overtake, but the product platform also builds a barrier of entry to new small players. It is very common for enthusiastic venture managers starting to pitch their new product supposed to replace an existing solution, to underestimate the resisting force of platform procurement viscosity and the long replacement cycles in big companies that already have supplier relationships in place. It takes a disruptively attractive offering to break through such barriers, and even so, takes time. Let's not forget that the customer is used to the current product in use. Furthermore, the customer has perhaps made a lot of adaptations and customizations making the product uniquely useful for the customer. All those adaptations may have to be redone from scratch if replacing the current product for a new product from another vendor. Add to all this also the community of current users, the investments made in learning the current product, and the flock effect that can delay making any change, despite having more information about defects as well as alternatives.

So, taken together, the vendor of the current product need not overly fear that an increased openness about shortcomings or advantages with the product in use will immediately have to lead to losing clients.

In consumer markets, decision cycles are of course shorter and therefore they can open up quicker for new ideas to break in. But people are habitual creatures, so even here the replacement speed can be lower can expected. This leads to the conclusion that not only new entrants, but also the market leader benefits from having an open dialogue with customers and other stakeholders.

In 2006, Chris Anderson of Wired Magazine blogged on this shift from away from secrecy, and highlighted:

> "Not just transparency, but Radical Transparency. The whole product development process laid bare, and opened to customer input".

The expected immediate gut reaction of the reader to this immoderate way, was immediately countered with the comment:

> "The small cost of some competitor getting early wind of a new feature is more than outweighed by the good will generated among customers by candid insights into product development."

Eight years after Anderson's comment, repeat findings in A.T. Kearney's 2014 Strategy Study[35] show that the secrecy reaction and its frustrations are as common as ever, and comments one manager interviewed:

> "The C-suite is afraid competitors will learn our strategy and so do not involve middle-level managers as much as they should in developing the strategy. Clearly, keeping our organization as much

---

[35] Aurik, J., Fabel, F., and Jonk, G. (2014)

in the dark as our competitors about our strategy is
not a fast lane to success."

To some extent, it is part of the role of a middle-lever
manager to be frustrated in the hierarchy squeeze and
contradictory goals, but I will apportion some
sympathy for a special disappointment if managers are
not feeling   at least a little informed on the
organization's direction via constant internal
communications and activities, in any case more than
competitors or the general public are.

6

Hard Work for Clarity

Transparency not only requires openness but also clarity, in order to become meaningful. Clarity does not come by itself through magic, but as the result of hard work.

As the networks of supply chains, international support teams, globally operating customers, and multi-channel marketing, all keep expanding and also becoming more and more entangled, this can cause an almost nauseous feeling for a customer or employee who is trying to make sense of all options available while having various information pointing in different directions. In this our modern age, instead of simplicity, it often feels as if we are facing a growing flow of input and opinions. Indeed, hundreds of daily decisions for an adult person today is to some extent about just that; not to jump to the first suggestion at its alleged face value, but evaluating if there is a need and mustering an appropriate amount of willpower to explore the actual options in a critical manner, and make a reasonably rational choice. Obviously, this applies for many everyday decisions we all face, like which utility to choose, which car to buy, which financing option to accept, etc. It would be foolish to claim that we behave that way all the time. Sometimes we do things that are knowingly irrational, to enjoy life, or spend less time evaluating other options because we're in a "shopping mode" and go with the flow. Even when we try really hard to be rational, our emotions and objectives get in between, more or less. Or like academics like to say, we are boundedly rational.

«»

With good intentions, lawmakers force companies to give more and more information to help consumers make more informed decisions, via "mandatory disclosure". It has grown especially quickly in the United States, because the concept resonates with American ideology principles of free-market choice and autonomous, informed consumers. Too much information pushed to the consumer to comply with regulations, can not only cause costs, but also provoke an even more irrational behavior, when cognitive limitations are hit, and a backlash in disclosure policy intent can occur.[36]. Which consumer has time or energy to read and understand all the user terms, consent forms, or all the small print in the whole pile of appendix papers? How many retirees with health problems are formally procuring their nursing home and doctors based on all available data?

People of all ages normally set aside only at most a reasonable amount of their available time and energy to each decision. This implies that few decisions are optimal, but many are good enough (this tactic is called "satisficing").

The following quote exemplifies the complexity that hits customers every day, and the tiredness it brings, even for highly trained recipients:

---

[36]Ben-Shahar and Schneider (2014) claim that mandatory disclosure is not necessarily an effective regulatory tool for the consumer market. According to the authors, the quantity and complexity of information, as well as consumers' cognitive limitations, are common reasons for failure of well-meaning disclosure policies.

"I teach contract law at Harvard, and I can't understand half of what it says."

Elizabeth Warren, former special advisor for the Consumer Financial Protection Bureau, about a consumer credit card agreement
text.[37]

To survive in this modern society, we employ satisficing tactics, or ignore things. In the workplace, the
expectations of rational behavior are (at least superfi-
cially) higher than at home. Actions by the office worker are supposed to have some rational meaning, to be
professional. When rule of thumb is used, it is based on
professional practice, and vocational training. Decisions, such as the selection of a vendor during a procurement, must in most cases pass through a process
of formalization and traceability.[38]

«»

Sometimes it is obvious what the most professional decision would be, but many times the parameters
are in a mist, or not possibly fully understandable, so
what is expected then?

Most assignments are received with even more
questions attached or arising, yet the assignee must get

[37] Quoted in Ben-Shahar, O., and Schneider, C.E. (2014) p.8.

[38] Re-weighting and scoring evaluation can sometimes be turned into a
long and complicated detour to select the candidate that intuitively felt
best all along anyway. Even so, there is some form of traceability.

to work immediately. The mass of uncertainties can temporarily paralyze even the most sturdy workhorse in these situations. Moreover, the avalanche of contradictory information from internal and external sources can be quite bad at the workplace nowadays, with heaps of messages coming rapidly from several directions at once. The tired look on some office workers can be the result of contradicting inputs just hitting them from different directions, typically from colleagues in different teams, or stakeholders basing their opinions on different grounds. When political struggle intervene in every single issue, a normal day can become tiresome, especially when the bombardment of other data continues without any pause. What hope for a mere human in all such contradictions?

There is hope. The first step is to see clearly the political tensions voiced, for what they are: conflicts of interests, more or less well-grounded. Therefore, be ready to use the political tools of compromising and negotiating to get anywhere, even if the assignment was not supposedly of a political nature at all. The second step is to prepare attacking major parts of the problem, as soon as they are possible to structure, and

begin make sense of the giant hairball, from understanding its main constituents.

«»

In this, it can be reassuring to remind oneself that
some of the most hairy parts are there, and has been
allowed to grow out of proportion, not to make the recipient feel helpless, but due to some stress or emulat-
ed handicap in previous link of the delivery chain that
made the matter arrive in such way.

To avoid stepping out of constricted mandate,
many employees skip even trying to simplify anything
while passing along work, because that contains a risk
of unwarranted removals or changes. It becomes artful
work-avoidance drilled in long chains. Hired expertise
help adding more smoke here and there. It is hardly
surprising that the overload of unstructured information makes decisions difficult, but it can be fairly effective to apply the mindset of an engineer and charge
ahead through the fog.

Bring a Sword

In engineering, there is a long tradition of fearlessly
attacking heaps of details. The idea is to not give in

even when the flood of incoming data is overwhelming, and the possible options seem to be just too many to choose from, but instead begin work by planning the battle: first contemplating how to generally attack that monster heap of details, then designing the analysis weapons that will begin to make sense of all the incoming data. The assumption underlying all this effort is of course that the design team will eventually win the battle of choices, and there will be balanced choices made, even when many routes are possible.

Apart from the data avalanche, there is sometimes a conceptual overload that can truly be intellectually challenging. For example, the "Dragon Book" is the nickname given to a university textbook[39] that, in its various editions[40], has been read by generations of computer science students. The main topic for that textbook is how to write a special piece of software (called a compiler) that reads a description of software from a text file (written by a human), and produces

---

[39] Written by Aho, Sethi, and Ullman, in 1986 (details are in the bibliography in the end).

[40] The first version, the "Green Dragon" book, was published already in 1977. Its successor, the "Red Dragon" took over in 1986. The red dragon reigned for two decades before retiring in 2006, supplanted with the 2nd edition; the "Purple Dragon" book.

machine instructions for a computer to run[41] The computer that will run the machine instructions can be the same computer that is reading the text file, but the software can just as well be prepared for later loading into another piece of equipment, e.g., an airplane, a dishwasher, or an internet router. For most students, grasping the essence of the compiler becomes mindwarping when the software for the compiler is written in the same programming language that the language it will then itself interpret. In the universe of symbol factories[42], the compiler is one that can eat itself[43] and reproduce. It may seem impossible to design something that can process itself in this way, but by attacking this challenge step-wise, it is quite possible, and we can see the successful results all around us in all electronic devices everywhere.

«»

[41] In 1951, Grace Hopper at Remington Rand, later U.S.Navy, invented the "compiler", writing the very first one known, for the "A0" language. See McGee, R.C. (2004), p.11.

[42] The fundamental symbol factory of course being mathematics. For example, in an intellectually exhausting attempt, Bertrand Russell and Alfred North Whitehead (1927), tried to formally construct mathematics from the bottom and up, introducing mathematical symbols and operators very carefully, and use this set of symbols to describe mathematics. Many famous mathematicians have attacked this challenge, both before and after this particular work, and continued to improve, and find flaws in these type of studies.

[43] This can also be exercised as an extreme example of the principle "Eating your own dog food". It has been told that when the IBM lab was developing

I will not slip deeper into computer science here, but allow me to make an observation: I have found it amusing to check for a common reaction of software engineers, when by chance of project work are handed copies of huge contracts of hundreds of pages written by commercial lawyers, with their signatory mesh of terminology and cross-references. Engineers do not feel the impulse to begin reading all the text, the way a lawyer would dig in. Rather, first ponder whether one can sketch a legal compiler that parses through the text and presents the key action points of it, with an automatically reorganized clarity of conceptual linking. The tool would have the sense to downplay minor definitions that already have solid traction in law and precedents, and bringing forth dangerous complications or contradictions in particular wordings that ought to be highlighted and discussed with the other party. Although a compiler idea is the first to pop up, to be really useful, such a contract assistance tool would need to have a library of all available grounding

the open-source Eclipse platform as an integrated developing environment for the Java language, the phrase 'eat our own dog food' was used frequently in the lab, in a positive sense (see http://c2.com/cgi/wiki?DogFood). The idea was that all the Eclipse developers use Eclipse every day, to do their own development for Eclipse on. The illustrative side benefit of making Eclipse as good as possible was that it simultaneously became a more powerful tool for developing Eclipse further.

for the jurisdictions involved so that it can process the text it was given and its inherent scenaria in a correctly composed atmosphere of not only statutory, regulatory, and common law. Obviously with calibrated expectation of *stare decisis.* So far, I haven't personally seen such a tool in use yet, but I do not think it would be anything strange.

The point is not although expertise will always be needed, useful tools have always been improving, and they will, in these areas, as in every other. Research and development is rapidly being made in semantic, multi-language technology. Automated text processors have already begun to help simplify, analyze, summarize, and translate large amounts of text in real time from multiple sources. These assisting tools will become more integrated into everyday workflows than we can even imagine now.

The "Dragon Book" got its nickname from its cover drawing that depicted a knight and a dragon in battle; a metaphor for conquering complexity. So, whenever that nauseous feeling of being overwhelmed creeps up, remember that hairy dragons do not have the willpower of a human, and can be slain. Then slowly pick up your sword.

Make Dragons Nicer

In modern society, there is unnecessary complexity hitting too many individuals, that could be swept up by revised public policy, without compromising ideals of free choice, and without going back to an opaque situation of yesteryear. I have noticed that many politicians fall into one of two extreme camps; one demands that government officials should decide for others what is best for them (i.e., no opt-out), the other camp insists that all people will, or should, prefer to make all detailed decisions by themselves about everything all the time (i.e., super-rational).

But the most convenient route for everyone, demands neither unrealistic super-rationality, nor an overly paternalistic stance.

Researchers Ben-Shahar and Schneider point out two major complexity cleaning methods[44] to make the dragons of modern life more timid, and thus nicer to meet with. The first method is the voluntary and simple delegation of details to experts to sort and feed-

---

[44] See Kai Falkenberg opinion column in Forbes Magazine (2010/0607).

back, and the second method is having a standard procedure of default choice.

As it is not possible to quickly make wise choices only based on long lists of facts, people need to have an easy and affordable way to delegate to appointed expertise; subject matter experts that take the consumers side, contextualize and simplify the choices in the best possible way.[45] The expert is not a real expert if the major possible choices are not presented lucidly. This will imply some filtering, but that is part of the simplification deal.

The other major cleaning method in the Ben-Shahar and Schneider recommendation is the fostering of practical and generally good decision making via channeling of possible choices into default options. This reduce the need of advance mandating for everything.

In other words, rule-makers in some areas of life carefully choose what can be the best option for most people, in average situations, and then let those who disagree to easily opt out from that default choice.

---

[45] Schneider exemplify this with expecting doctors recommend a course of action for the patient, and then allow discussion of reasonable alternatives. In all other daily interactions with representatives of suppliers and municipal boards, etc. The customer or patient or citizen, is to receive the benefits of calling for advice, and not just be thrown a heap of more or less unsorted information to digest and come up with an answer what to do.

Opting-out can be just ever so slightly, by fine-tuning the default choice, ranging to completely re-placing the default choice for something else, for whatever personal reason. The amount of replacement possibility can be limited for various reasons, deemed necessary to avoid extremes that would be politically or ethically unacceptable.

A classic example is the inheritance law of most countries around the world. Typically, people do not have to write their own will, as the default choice of spouse, children, etc. (details varying between states), then remain in effect. Such default choice is then a promoted decision by default.

«»

Another example of trying to combine free choice with an assisted decision by default, is when Sweden introduced a mandatory additional pension scheme, called the premium pension, where a fraction of income taxes are put into mutual funds, two principles were enforced in the program:

The first principle was that private fund management companies were invited to provide alternatives for placement of savings, but their fund management

fees was to be reduced for money that had been collected in bulk from income taxes, compared to charges
debited from individual investors.

The second principle was on the default choice:
those citizens who did not make an active choice of investment funds for their premium pension savings,
were instead given shares in a government-run pension fund.[46] At the moment (January 2015), 44% of the
citizens currently enrolled in the mandatory pension
scheme, remains in this default option.[47]

Interestingly, as of writing, the shares in the default fund has had a better outcome for the savers,
than the total average outcome of all active choices of
private alternatives made via the program.[48] So, in a
sense, no one can complain much about the overall setup: those citizens that were passive, for whatever reason, have not been short-changed. Those who used the
opportunity to make investment choices with a small
part of their retirement funds, and if those choices

---

[46] Currently, the "AP7 Såfa" fund is the default fund in the
Swedish premium pension system.

[47] See www.ap7.se

[48] For all pension savers as a group, and for the time window
2002-2014, according to comparison graph (available 2014-12-04)
at http://www.ap7.se/en/About-AP7/

turned out to be worse than average (or worse than the no choice option), at least this happened because of a voluntary move, and there was hopefully some joy in having the freedom to decide for oneself. Those who has made investment choices that has made their pension fund grow better than the default option, are supposedly happy to have been given that choice. As a twist to the story, the government-run fund remains on the list of possible alternatives, i.e., as a voluntary choice to opt-in.

At the time of writing, 857 alternatives[49] are open to choose from in the premium pension scheme. Citizens can choose up to ten funds and then decide the proportions between the funds, using their personal login at the pensions agency to direct their individually tagged contribution.

The critique against the scheme was not on the default choice (as it has proven well-calibrated thus far), but on the overload of data to regular citizens, most of whom do not enjoy analyzing investment portfolio parameters. There was some pre-filtering of allowed choices from the funds universe because of the pro-

---

[49] The list can be reviewed any time at http://secure.pensionsmyndigheten.se/SokFonder.html

curement criteria, and there was of course the rebate on fund management fee, but allegedly there was not enough of a built-in layer where subject matter experts took the consumers side and simplified matters further. In accordance with consumer market logic, the roll-out therefore immediately opened an opportunity for unserious so-called advisors to sweep in, and use all typical telemarketing tricks to make money from their victims. Even citizens who had basic education in investment fundamentals, refused unserious advice, and went for an active choice, can very easily fail to put an appropriate balance and time horizon on their allocation choices, and inject much higher risks into their pension portfolio than an institutional pension fund manager would.

Also, no matter how well-designed the list of choices on the agency web site, incrementally became (last time I checked it looked better than those at most banks), for most citizens, the practical task of making detailed choices for a personalized premium pension portfolio, appeared just as another modern day little dragon[50], to ignore or keep at bay with minimal effort.

---

[50] As is the case with every politically controlled pool of money, where citizens are given some degree of self-control in the short term, the big question is not whether a percentage here and there

Moving on a bit from the effort needed to slay dragons, and the mess created by laziness of not even trying to, it now feels natural to passably explore organizational backwardness.

Overcoming Organizational Stupidity

Unfortunately, with increased mental and social pressures at work, there is no clear-cut evidence that workplace relations in general are really getting much better over the last decades.

On the contrary, some researchers believe that objectively studying emotions at the workplace is as important as ever, to investigate elements of social toxicity, such as belittling of others (especially if it is used as part of management culture), and other phenomena such as ignorance, vanity, and organizational stupidity.[51]

---

are optimally allocated by individuals. Overarching that is the political fact that no-one knows how the future of the whole program will develop over time, due to demographic tilts, surrounding macro forces, and political shifts. Intuitively, many citizens avoid spending too much time on any self-administration setup where there is no guarantee that tagged money will still be actually available to withdraw thirty years later.

[51] A summary on this area of research can be found in the preface of Lemmergaard and Muhr (2013).

In the social aspects of workplace life, facing manager's prestige maneuvers and surrounding massive power-play games, the challenges for an office worker are seldom so crisp as in a well-defined engineering task.

Contradictions between many incoming requests, and a pressure to do many tasks at once, quickly become stressful. Most office staff realize that the only way to survive a typical week at work, is to first see that it's completely impossible to keep everyone happy all the time. Moreover, there is seldom any point in over-delivering. Surviving in jobs today, requires an acceptance of mediocrity, i.e., to calibrate a certain amount of resignation but without causing irritation, and perform this with graceful disregard of mildly insulting components packed into some orders. One example can be a forced task of having to formally re-apply for one's current position during a reorganization. The employees that are still passably awake, rightly question the real reason for such a procedure step.

《》

On a positive note, after overcoming a challenging task of information processing in the workplace, and if the social outcomes are also alright, there is the benefit of gaining a piece of additional self-confidence and more encouragement to take on the next challenge. Coalitions can be formed, and teams become stronger by challenges and small victories. Just like the negative spiral of unemployment, there is the positive spiral of completing things and moving along. The main challenge in surviving in the office of today, is to decide exactly when to apply energy in a burst effort, and when to await patiently that some matters stabilize a bit more.

To help staff make all their daily decisions about how to spend their energy more wisely, nothing beats letting experience combine with insight. Do not leave colleagues in the dark. Show your cards, display what is at hand, be frank about the obstacles in your project. Suddenly, unexpected help may be on its way.

The major organizational stupidity emerges where troubles and mistakes are covered-up, and keeping face is everything. A lot of fancy footwork is then spent on pretense pirouettes, making the whole organization dance according to a defensive pattern[52] in which everyone is busy looking at their own backs, instead of looking ahead where they are going.

In such a smoggy organization, dialogue becomes twisted into sophisticated nonsense. As a contrast, working in a transparent corporation is characterized by direct speech and good visibility.

---

[52] Best described by Chris Argyris (1990).

Part II
THE CUBIC
DIMENSIONS OF
ENTERPRISE

7

Products

With "products", we mean whichever artifact or service that is satisfying a customer need, generating customer value, and without which the corporation has no reason to exist. Everything the corporation is doing, is supposed to be supporting its product delivery. Only by satisfactory delivery of products, will there be any sustainable revenue at all.

In the following description, keep in mind that products are not only physical goods, but whatever it is that the corporation provides in any form to its customers. Services (standardized, or ad-hoc), are often part of the product offering, or they are, in fact, the only product. The   customer value of the "total prod-uct", can be envisioned rising up vertically along the product axis, and it is construed from three accumu-lating levels: "core" product, "actual" product, and "augmented" product[53]. In a visualization, we plot this total generation of customer value in the vertical di-rection, so the vertical side of the Glass Cube will rep-resent 100% of the currently generated customer value (or a proxy for that value)[54].

Although it is the proportional blend that is of in-terest in this display, one can also put grading labels on the axis. To simplify, the snapshot measurement can be the current sales income, per the shortest rea-sonable time period, i.e., accrued revenue on an in-come statement. This is based on the simple premise that economic compensation from customers is the easiest assessment of value generation. In special situa-tions, where sales revenue is not available or relevant, the product axis plot can be made in another appropri-

---

[53] Here, we follow in the footsteps of Theodore Levitt, founder of modern marketing.

[54] In this discussion, we assume that the intent is good. A scam product has very low, zero, or even negative customer value. Some Black Blob companies build up the image of a proper commercial activity, but deliver useless or nearly useless products, a fact which they try to cover up with cosmetics and more or less creative lies.

ate measurement of fulfillment of customer stakeholder objectives.

When assessing the economics of a corporation,
income streams from sales are the very first numbers
to check, and from which costs will be subtracted for
the basic profit-loss analysis. Or, as management guru
Drucker once proclaimed: the No.1 job of the executive
is to manage the business for economic performance.[55]
Granted, there are innumerous flaws if using current
revenues as a representation of customer value generation, both in the short and long term, but deprived of
an easier way to capture a meaningful expression of
customer value having any stronger signal strength,
this is accepted as, if not the definitive measurement, a
proxy for customer value generation[56].

«»

---

[55] Drucker (1954) on general management.

[56] Note that it is expressed customer value related to satisfaction
of a need (genuine or fictional), that is captured in this measurement. Whether the consumption is objectively meaningful, actually helpful, or healthy for the subject, is not the concern at this
particular point. Whether society as a whole receive any net
benefits from the product delivery is also sometimes very ques-
tionable. Nevertheless, to allow for a model in simple form, we
must be careful not to pass judgment on customer value observa-
tions. This matter is comparable to the debate on measuring of

In the Glass Cube image of an enterprise, the concept of a product line can be illustrated visually by placing the two or more related product stacks near each other. The plots for an individual product can be made in layers to illustrate bundled parts, or only for the whole as one consolidated pillar. The particulars of componentization, the value attributed to core product and to other components of the total product delivery, are articulated in module price lists, internal pricing sheets, or can be sketched from estimated contribution degrees to the total product. The sales modules are the contributors of interest in the product value perspective, not the technical components. Based on this understanding of, and intention with, the total product, the product manager reviews customer opinions, competitive research, as well as profit-loss calculations of modules in offerings, and then designs pricing schemes together with the sales and marketing staff. Again, remember that the total product includes everything that the customer receives or experiences, also intangibles, endorsements, and brand values. So, there are two entrepreneurial functions in a corporation that act

---

gross national product.

intensely along the product axis: innovation and marketing[57].

With the innovation function acting on the product axis, I do not mean simply with idea generation activity. Any group of people can generate miscellaneous
ideas; that is seldom a challenge. It is well understood
that the routines in place in an established enterprise
for efficient and safer operations, will intentionally (or
as a side-effect) suffocate creativity. In most business
operations, some lack of creativity is neither such a big
problem on an ordinary day, nor such an easy fix, as
some cheerful speakers tend to propagate at annual
kick-off events. This particular lock-down to focus on
current problem-solving, is not a disease to be cured,
it is the name of the game. However, when a complex
organization eventually starts putting resources behind something, there are know-how and resources to
implement and follow-through with the initiative, of-

---

[57] Note that in the Glass Cube Strategy, the defining part of the
product-market mix, is the product line, rather than customer
segments. This is due to the fact that the customer marketplace is
not something under the company's control: the customers are a
crucial part of the environment with which the company interact,
but customer segments are of course not corporate assets (no
matter how much contract lock-in and retention effort is
engaged).

ten leading to more chances of success than when a solo ideator is acting creatively in the spur of a moment. Or in the words of a marketing director[58]: "The hard part of innovation isn't coming up with an idea; rather it's picking the right one to develop".

For the product owner, the hard choice is organizing various lists and picking the right idea to develop first, or which maintenance to undertake soonest, and these decisions are based on a deep understanding of current product platform and customer value generation possibilities. When a corporation does decide on a course, it can get to work. In the Glass Cube, this power is illustrated by the base of resources and operations, a matrix that can accomplish many things at once, which we will see more of in the next chapters.

Type of value generated

As discussed, the value generated along the product axis, is relatively obvious. As any sales executive will be quick to remind you, revenues from products and

---

[58] Quoted in Agan (2014).

services are brazenly incoming figures. In the most blatant form, it is hard cash into accounts receivable.

But appreciated deliveries also create goodwill-building, increase brand recognition, build respect and curiosity from current or prospective customers, and pump other types of popularity points for the short and long run.

Although sometimes in such immaterial shape, all the work invested along the product axis is supposed to turn into revenue one day, in one way or another.[59]

To allow for start-ups that do not yet have any sales at all, and no signed customer yet, but wish to implement a Glass Cube Strategy, then (with extreme caution) the product axis can contain a plot of an R&D-artifact, where the customer stakeholder is represented by prospects, and the value generation plot is approximated with a placeholder for the product expressed ei-

---

[59] If no compensation, we are seeing consumption rather than production. Apart from masked consumption, the other options for activities taking place along the product axis but without genuine hope of future revenue, would be corruption-driven setups. Bleeding out of incompetence is not a crime, but if someone is funneling vital resources from a corporation, without any purpose of conserving or expanding the product axis, and without such actions being part of orderly disinvestment (or a managed bankruptcy procedure), that person has entered the shadowy lands of *abus-de-confiance.*

ther as an opportunity cost on an accrual basis, or in terms of discounted cash inflows for its corresponding real option, in either case with reasoned judgment[60] and for the same assessment period used for plots on the other axes.

Product Strategy

The product strategy is a major part of formulating an idea on how to create value for the customer. This sounds straightforward enough, but without very vigilant care, the product strategy slowly degenerates. Step by step it becomes filled with contradictions, confusions, outdated descriptions, and various vague statements; in short, creating many new problems that are cumbersome even for long-time employees to disentangle, and in the absolutely worst case, the whole problem set is then bounced back to the customer to figure out !

As can be seen in numerous examples during the last centuries of business, simplicity is a major success factor. As a consequence, the product strategy must be

---

[60] A good guide to these concepts is the International Good Practice Guidance by IFAC (2013).

easily understandable to be efficient. An understandable product strategy often have an air of great and beautiful simplification around it, that looks like the only obvious way - in hindsight. Choosing to ultra-focus on something for a better and more precise effect, means leaving many other things out, and that can be a tough call. But it is a call that has to be made.

In an engineering or manufacturing company, the product itself can be a real-world artifact, that we can touch and feel. In comparison, a government agency can have difficulty defining what its (intangible) product is, and also for whom it is actually delivered. In some situations, the "customer" can be a mesh of stakeholders. Using the word "customer" too directly, can become outright ridiculous in some cases, like when a penitentiary used it for its prisoners, which is a rather inverted statement[61].

To reiterate; sometimes, there is no individual or distinct organization that is a direct beneficiary of what the organization is doing. Nevertheless, every corporation produces a product (however abstract it

---

[61] I doubt that the prisoners *chose* to check in at that particular prison establishment, after having duly done their consumer research on a "JailAdvisor" website. On the contrary: the real customer of jails, is rather society *except* the detainee.

might be), and to a customer (however abstract it may be). Without a product strategy to govern upcoming work, random factors will come to influence what will happen next, so there will be no consistency in the work or in the selections made. Soon enough, customers and other stakeholders will lose confidence, not only in the product line, but in the venture as a whole.

Note that the product strategy can be extremely simple, even blunt, but it has to be there.

Road Map as Ambitious Compromise

Traditionally, the focus of product planning in a mass-market economy, was the three steps of combining a market segmentation (understanding the customer) with a selection of solution (solving the problem), managing the requirements, and pricing the product. Increasingly, businesses are now building a more sophisticated and forward-looking forecasting of needs, i.e. describing the challenge before it has fully arisen.

This planning work is fed with input from product portfolio steering, analysis of technology and market trends, but also by identifying what troubles the customers are facing now and what new challenges are waiting around the corner.

Sometimes the assets available in product platforms, operational competence, and current resources, need to be reorganized in creative ways to provide for upcoming products. The biggest challenge for a product manager is then to overcome harsh internal resistance against messing with what works. Part of product planning is therefore the change management needed to really prove the soundness and viability of the product strategy themes, and make sure that the business logic is water tight. The most ardent critics of radical product reengineering should be the experts on the current product and the versions that are in practical use today.

All these inputs come together into the product roadmap that shows the nature of upcoming vital lifecycle events, version releases, and other main product events, on a timeframe for the product plan up to a planning horizon set at anything between one and five years ahead.

Although some simplifications can be made in the basic product planning regarding time-to-market criticalities, a product strategy must take into account a competitive analysis to form a road-map: the crux of a roadmap is this timing of market and technology. Taking a bet on themes and assets, and when they become available for delivery, is very hard - but must be done anyway. The best guesstimates for future launch dates and what they mean, are illustrated in the road map.

«»

When choosing between different possible options for the product's future, the organization meant to realize the product strategy is not a silent backdrop to the planning game. On the contrary, product managers are practically immersed in the organization's culture, and with close consideration of conflicting ambitions and modus operandi. So, product managers make tacit decisions on product strategy based on their experiences of and outlook of the organization that will develop, deliver, and maintain the product going forward.

The road map is not a dream scenario, but the deliberate result of thousands of filtering choices, decisions, and compromises, that had to be made beginning from blue-sky ambitions.

Road Map for Wider View

It is striking how every problem-solving organization gets better day by day in applying its favorite solutions, but simultaneously lose sight of adjacent areas. This "crystallized competence" is the result of accumulating many small steps, each by itself rational, into an impressively focused but restricted attention.

Sometimes, an add-on to a current product was designed in a certain way mainly because the organization happened to have a department or team specialized in that area, available when needed. In other words, the product structure will always to some extent mirror the organizational structure, and vice versa. This interplay can be subtle in its smaller steps, even for the people involved. Over time, the problem-solving organizational structure is therefore a result of a conceptual product structure that has evolved from thousands of previous product management decisions, and overall corporate history. Inevitably, inertia within the organization poses limits on what changes can be achieved along the product axis[62].

«»

A corporation that survived its start-up phase, and that has grown into a mature firm, had to perform many ritualistic and repetitive behaviors over the years, and come to show an obsessive interest in the product area.

Nevertheless, to retain some peripheral vision is crucial in product strategy work. To find an appropriate balance between keeping a harsh focus and widening the outlook, is a constant major challenge for any product manager who is handling a mature product, not only because its a difficult act in itself, but because there are tremendous internal corporate forces in play. The reward circuitry towards the workforce, in much of corporate culture today is driven by paying salary and bonus to employees according to communicated goals, and also complemented with other rewards for displaying shared loyalty to selected objects of inter-

---

[62] This inertia often forms the hardest challenge for product managers that are sensing the urge to respond to competitive pressure, see Gulati & Eppinger (1996).

est, and to relentlessly stay on topic. People have some moral compass but the corporation as such does not have to show much social responsibility unless forced by law, and as a legal person can have difficulty forming and sustaining genuine partnerships, make clumsy moves now and then, and tend to stick to its routines whatever the circumstance. Every corporation eventually become myopic about its products and interests, and show great pride in its chosen focus, even when that focus is outdated or misguided. Taken together, one of the hallmarks of a mature corporation is that its general behavior becomes what could be provokingly described as autistic[63].

Pitfall: Problem transfer, disguised as educating the customer

Do you also get a slightly uneasy feeling when you go somewhere for information on a product, and the ser-

---

[63] This was said with whole-hearted respect for individuals having any form of autism spectrum disorder, also, with full sympathy to families taking emotional tolls in their daily life, while caring for a family member. The comparison was only in one direction, and only as a thought starter on corporate personae in this particular context. The reward circuitry function in humans has been investigated by Dichter et al. (2012).

vice provider robotically begins to educate you, before even attempting to respond to the actual question? Although it is worst when happening in person, it can also be mildly annoying to meet this tone on a website. No customer has to accept being talked down to with a patronizing tone. I love learning, but prefer to do it in my way by seeking my various sources, before making a decision. It is unlikely that I would use the seller as the only source of information, but I appreciate all friendly pointers to other external and trustworthy sources for further research. There is a fine balance between a seller showing passion and interest, and a seller that seek grandiosity at the customer's expense. It is quickly obvious if, instead of helping me making my buying decision easier, the seller uses the opportunity to glorify the seller's competence, as if competitors are nonexistent. If it is not clear to me as a customer anyway that the proposed design is obviously better, or that the price list is attractive, then I don't need argumentation for it either; such maneuvers only turns into an overall sentiment that if I just listen up better, I will have to agree to the splendor. Of course, customers sometimes need guidance, and when done respectfully, helpfulness is a truly positive experience.

In contrast, telling me that I expressed my need in the wrong way, is not nice education. Having a sellers view of own importance forced upon me, is also not a very nice experience. But if you can display good examples of what you do well, and how that can help people that are in my situation, I will certainly listen. All attempts of educating the customer needs fingerspitzengefühl to be enjoyable and lead to more business. So, the major pitfall is this: to transfer a complicated problem back to the customer, and pretend it is in the customers best interest all along to have some of the core problem pushed back. Especially when simultaneously obfuscating the real price model, and finally, making comparisons with other vendors harder instead of easier.

«»

This method is still surprisingly common in financial services, with house mortgages conditions and similar. Naively, one would assume that a bank is an expert in what to do; calibrating interest rate swaps and applying portfolio risk control, and will use those skills, and the financial muscles of the institute behind the scenes, to make the end customer's choice super-clear and easily comparable, and without any hidden excuses.

All too often, the complete opposite happens; problems are transferred back to the customer, risks are silently shifted, and price conditions kept purposefully nontransparent and extremely hard, if not impossible, to evaluate in advance in the competitive space on quickly comparable terms.

«»

If the seller wishes to abdicate from the procurement simplification problem I came to seek the seller's help with, then it infuriates me when this is done by pretending to disguise the problem transfer as an education. I immediately translate such lectures into something more like "if you only knew how hard our job is, you would never ask for our help to solve your problem and present a couple of clear-cut options for you. Also, being such a complicated space, do not expect any possibility to compare our offering with anything from any other vendor. Sure, you can try set up your own comparison model, but it will take you weeks, and it will be impossible without having our level of expertise in the first place".

Well, dear solution provider, try harder. If you really are good, and can truly *simplify* my life, then prove it. *That* will make me a loyal client.

8

Operations

The Second Strategic Question:

How to differentiate in the *way* to create value?

Now, we will explore the second axis: "operations". With operations, we take the widest definition of all activities in the corporation; we include all the ongoing production work, all coordination efforts, research & development, plus the corporate functions.

The wish-list from customers, channeled through account managers and product managers, should (in a healthy enterprise with thriving customer relations) always be longer than what the mustered resources can create without delay.

So the organization has therefore institutionalized the resulting   permanent internal conflict for resources into the famous two-dimensional "project-resource-matrix".

As we will see below, the project-resource-matrix is where the hierarchic line organization that musters resources, interplay[64] with the operations organization that produces results and changes.

Type of value generated

The value generation of the operations axis is the fulfillment of deliveries to the product market, the development and preparations work needed for and intending to fulfill upcoming deliveries towards the product market in the future, and the coordinated corporate functions that makes the corporation operate.

Traditionally, companies have organized the bulk of labor into work-flows and further into tasks, and many of these tasks have been repeated almost every

---

[64] In Drucker's words, the 2nd job of management is to "manage managers" (to make resources productive and build an organization), and the 3rd job is to "manage workers and work". We simplify these two statements into "managing operations".

workday, sometimes many times per day. The hierarchic line organization executing tasks is the classic definition of operations, but in fact this cluster of line tasks is simply the beginning point of an operations axis, that in today's environment is a full spectrum of assignment-horizons passing from tasks, via missions, and to the domain of projects. Nowadays, a person typically will have to switch between executing work-flow tasks in line operations, and tasks in one or several projects, and these switches can occur many times per day.

Borders between line operations tasks and project operations tasks are often blurry and have to be adjusted on an ongoing basis. It is important that this dialogue between project managers and line managers is held in a routine way with neutral voice, being a core part of organizational life. Uncorrected and escalated irritation over the normal friction that is naturally occurring along the interfaces between line and project work, is not constructive. The best style is to let every employee detect and state ambiguities immediately as they are arising, and (as much as possible) be given space to resolve scheduling conflicts in a matter-of-fact dialogue, case by case. Escalating conflicts until they are resolved. All lowest-level-possible decisions on "who-does-what" should then be documented on a formalization level that is minimally acceptable to both the line and the various projects: the simplest crisp and unbureaucratic fashion that can be found and shared, that will avoid irritation on repeatedly resurfacing scheduling issues.

Matrix Battlefield

The ongoing internal battles in the project-resource-matrix is all too well-known for everyone who have ever worked in an office at some point, during the last forty years or so. In fact, most officers nowadays spend a significant amount of their career in a series of daily, monthly, and annual skirmishes in exactly that matrix. Handling that game well, i.e., without gaining too many enemies, often leads to promotion.

My suggestion is that the next time you visit a steering committee, take a good look around the table, and you will see people with hard-won experiences of the political slings and arrows of thousands of resourcing conflicts. As we will discuss below, managing the project-resource-matrix is crucial for an efficient organization, so it is no wonder that people with any aptitude for this, rapidly advance up the echelons.

Many professionals who reach this step in their career experience a mix of ennui with a feeling that something is basically wrong. It can be heard by the oozing comments, filled with acid insights from too many previous petty conflicts. The particular air of battle fatigue can be an almost attractive factor for the other managers, who find it very befitting, and cements the tired officer's apparent suitability to sit also in the next steering committee, to hear and produce some more acid comments. In the midst of this virtual combat, professionals wonder if their organization is actually the absolutely worst one on the planet, but correctly realize it must be more or less the same sort of troubles over at the competitor's camp; that their grass is equally... grey.

Three Execution Styles within Operations

As mentioned, activities are grouped with different planning horizons and organized in different fashion. Specific activities along the Operations axis basically take place primarily within one of three execution styles: process, missions, or projects. Most corporations are simultaneously operating hundreds of linked processes, many parallel missions, and several interdependent projects. This will be important to remember when we introduce the principle of "Open Status" in Part III.

Process

All the relatively routine work taking place in the corporation we classify as process tasks. A task does not have to be simple, in itself it can require a very highly trained skill, and focused attention. But uncertainties surrounding the task, about its impact on the rest of the organization, is normally limited, therefore the coordination needs with other activities is limited and/or well-defined. Most tasks can be executed by one or two people, and completed within a day. Tasks tend to recur, based on calendar or repeating events, and there are many good reasons to have agreed processes and to find ways to support and administer tasks, so that the workflow can proceed smoothly and minimize errors.

One challenge surrounding tasks, is that the details in the processes are ever-changing because the environment is ever-changing. This can irritate employees as constant changes goes against the "promise" of setting up, training for, and optimizing a task-based process. For obvious reasons, the operations staffers want the process to stay fixed, but project work and revisional processes are constantly changing the details of said process, and at times it can be hard to keep up with all the revised routines.

Another challenge is that as the routines are automated, boredom can lead to fatigue and inattention. To monitor a machine doing its work, is normally not difficult, but it is passivizing, and then when something suddenly happens without warning, the time it takes to get hold of controls, can be long.

«»

It is also deceptive that task automation would remove physical danger. Normally, it reduces hazards, but the one remaining can be just as dangerous. For example, even if the advanced deforestation machines that are roaming the forests in countries like Sweden are generally safe, forest work is still a relatively hazardous occupation. The task of moving in the terrain in huge machines and cutting down trees with sharpened chains has inherent risks.

Another example that could illustrate this point, is a scene in the 2013 science-fiction movie Elysiem, where a worker had to enter a piece of automated manufacture machinery, and was badly hurt. The movie takes place in the year 2154, when – supposedly - the very wealthy live on a space station, while the rest of the population resides on a ruined Earth. Task automation had apparently not removed physical danger at all workplaces, even by then.

Finally, I must also mention the new risks arising when task automation, that can make a process both easier and safer than with manual operation, hits complex failures, it quickly becomes more dangerous than if the process had been under full manual control at the failure. A common scenario is when there are data input errors combining with operator misunderstanding, and a lack of time to recover and regroup back to normal. Recent sad examples from commercial aviation, especially AF447 in 2009, are on top of mind, and should be studied in depth by everyone who work with task automation, in any industry. But commercial aviation is also the greatest inspiration in this area, with impressive results from all the persistent safety work done for over a century, ever since the first scheduled service[65] began in January, 1914.

Most tasks within operations are not dangerous at all, but administrative in nature, typically with very limited physical or economic consequences should anything go wrong once in a while. Nevertheless, studying the what happens when tasks go into exception mode and collude to enter a critical chain of events, is always worthy of studying, at least for the work-flows that are businesses-critical in a corporation. Luckily, the consequences of problems and task failures, are seldom leading to fatalities, injuries, or even bankruptcy.

An important takeaway from studying the mechanics of task confusion and team disarray under severe pressure, is that teamwork based on a "results & safety"-culture with a strong emphasis of situation-effective communication about the current state of the

---

[65] IATA Press Release: "New Year's Day 2014 marks 100 Years of Commercial Aviation", see www.iata.org/pressroom/pr/Pages/2013-12-30-01.aspx

mission, matters more than individual skills in specific tasks. This leads us into the next style of operations.

Mission

The intermediate style of operations consists of missions. In a sense, executing missions well - and repeatedly so - forms the apex of operational excellence; because missions are more complex than tasks, but not as unique as projects. It means that a corporation can become very good at executing missions, build a reputation from that, and its customers can have a fairly good sense of what to expect of the next mission.

A mission is a grouping of tasks into relatively well-known families of sequences that are applied to achieve specific targets. Unless some extraordinary circumstance adversely affects the mission, the predefined target will be reached, and the customers will be pleased with that.

In established corporations, carefully designed routines have been developed to reduce risks during the mission, and the teams have practiced similar missions before, so there is a domain-specific competence built-up both in the organization and in all the teams.

It even becomes a culture, with many stories to tell, and a colorful jargon. The more similar successful missions that a team member has partaken in previously, the more tacit knowledge is gained. Techniques are practiced, and mission commanders become skillful in reorienting tasks quickly depending on how the mission evolves, to separate important from less important events in the mission context. Surprises will come in every mission, big and small, but drawing from experiences, most problems can be solved or circumvented, to continue towards the goal of the mission.

The need of coordination between missions are of a relatively predictable nature, and tend to be part of the routine tasks packages. Although some conflicts that can happen between missions, the overall need of mission separation is clear to everyone participating in either mission.

During the launch coordination to get the mission going, and in the hand-off procedure in the completion and closing, the mission is created from line resources and then dismantled into line resources again. This happens in parallel and in sequence with other missions, so mission timing is crucial. The corporation builds up methods for thorough resource planning, and there is a deep and natural coordination between mission planning and line resourcing.

If process and mission coordination is intense, interestingly,   inter-mission coordination enroute is more ad-hoc, perhaps helping out if possible when a parallel mission needs some assistance, but in general the important messages and contacts between missions are about not colliding with another mission[66]. The inter-mission coordination is in fact mostly to avoid unintentionally   obstructing - or in the worst case destroying - a parallel mission[67]. Apart from that, each mission is on its own while it is ongoing.

Project

Finally, the third style of operations, the one with the least proportions of repeated types of decisions, is called Projects.

Of course, there are many routines and many stretches of tedious work in projects; actually a lot of

---

[66] Sometimes referred to as "conflict resolution"

[67] Unintended destruction could happen when there are too quick decisions together with dangerous misinformation or accumulated misunderstandings (in extreme cases this is a so-called "friendly fire" situation)

project work can be more tedious than mission work is, but the project as a whole is more difficult to plan (and replan) than tasks or missions.

One misconception about projects is that they have been invented to make some activities happen in a coordinated way in an organization (and along the way pass some milestones to give a sense of progress and control).

Firstly, more frequent and more highly skilled everyday coordination is much better seen between process tasks or between missions, and you can study how they use more of standard vocabulary for their coordination. Between a project and other projects (and all other operations), more apparently unique situations tend to arise, with more difficulties to analyze and explain dependencies. It is not unusual that part of the coordination problem is due to unaccustomed or unstable vocabulary in the situations encountered by the project. Many of the situations are not so unique at all, in a more abstract sense, but to the participants it seems that many of the particular problems are happening for the first time. The control structure for projects are installed to work these challenging factors, spending energy on the headwind met because projects are not line tasks. To shovel line tasks or missions onto the project style of operations, is therefore very counterproductive.

Moreover, a project is not created from its activities. Instead, it is the reaching of a specified and unique outcome that is the reason for creating a project, and everything else is a set of practicalities. Only those activities designed to maximize utility towards the uniquely sought outcome, at the particular time of project execution, and as best judged in the representational project plan[68], shall exist in the project. Any attempt to create projects from predetermined activities, is therefore plainly misguided.

The particular outcome set forth in the project directive has not been sought before in the organization, and will never be the same in the future either. In comparison, a mission can be repeated with similar resources another day, if the environment did not change too much overnight. This desire of repeatability is not the case with a project.

---

[68] Wheres the baseline plan is the project owners' original order, and the nominal plan is the currently valid order from the steering committee, the representational plan is the project manager's own daily judgment of detailed status, particular progress, and all deviations. See Cleden (2012), p.31.

Along the operational scale between tasks, via missions, to projects, the "before-start" uncertainties and the "during execution" uncertainties, are gradually higher for each operational style.

In tasks and missions, the resources practice and strive for execution excellence: combining high throughput of correct quality, with readiness for unplanned events. In this readiness, a smooth flexibility within the given frames are part of the operational skills. A mission commander, after a lot of training and experience, is expected to handle stressful situations with skilled prioritization and resoluteness.

The same niveau of operational brilliance is not to be expected from project managers. On the other hand, projects need to maneuver within unknown frames, getting through ambiguous days when neither the situation nor the destination are understood. The "management" of uncertainties is therefore at the core of project management[69], and in this task, project managers need to display a special professionalism.

---

[69] See p.37 in Cleden (2009).

Pitfall: Complicating the organization to make people feel important

In some organizations, handing out titles is easier than fixing a problem (or rise the salary), and most staff respond well to the inflation in titles. But satisfaction from job titles is short-lived, so it is therefore a zero-sum game of chasing transient status markers.

This can happen in every style of operations, but because missions have a stronger culture around fixed roles, it is more common and more amusing to study in the process line organization or in the project organization. Let us study the pitfall as it occurs in the projects. Without balancing this inflation tendency, a completely normal project can turn out to have not only one project manager, but something like three or four; given various names like "Business-PM", "Implementation PM", "IT-Project Manager", and so on. Then, of course, the original PM will have to be renamed into more and more pompous terms; "Main PM", "Lead PM", "Head PM", "Project Director", etc. In parallel, what used to be activity groups or small teams, inflate into sub-projects, and then to projects. Not to stop there, the normal-sized or larger projects becomes programs, and the previous programs need to be strategic programs, and so on, and so forth. It is not only a game with words. During this juggling, hairy bombs of coordination disaster are mounted.

Not that title inflation itself matters – why not let everyone alive be the president of something - but when the originally simple control structure of a project is replaced by vague other vocabulary (that no-one really understands how to apply in practical situations), there will be some real confusion arising. That confusion cause braking friction and then in the end results in apathy on the floor when project members perceive the increasing disconnect between command line reports and orders, and what is actually happening in the daily work.

Everyone wants to avoid routine tasks, but increasingly there also is an avoidance of tasks that demands cognitive effort. Few are content being the simple footman pulling ahead, especially when it becomes obvious that success gets disconnected from fulfilling true work tasks. People have a basic human need to feel valuable in their jobs, but the lesson of trapping in this pitfall, is that this value can not be faked through the project organization, in projects, there need to be genuinely good progress, and truly working and useful output. For a project, nothing else should matter, so it is not an appropriate scene for shows without substance.

To reverse the trend of malfunctioning grandiosity, requires an executive order of "back-to-basics": forcing leaner control structures and shorter, simpler projects that deliver actual results that quickly can be of use. Such a major "reset" to basic project principles can certainly be combined with revised concepts for project portfolio metrics, and reinvigorating of an effect-focused view of project steering. There are cases when, e.g., the program concept makes sense, and then it should be used, otherwise not.

I believe it is important to periodically reinstate a renewed respect within each and every corporation for a positive "roll-up-the-sleeves" attitude of getting things done. And that, in many cases, projects are a good setting for precisely that.

The fundamental problem of unsatisfactory work needs to be addressed head on, with great openness and humor, with the (for the most part) talented, educated, and loyal professionals. Allowing some of the more opportunistic persons   to manipulate project structures to play self-images, only leads to widespread skepticism, and a permanently reduced output of useful results. To avoid this pitfall, an enterprise should pursue purposeful metrics of project steering accomplishment, as well as process and mission statistics, and with childish honesty point out whenever the clothes misfit or are missing. Apart from in a good bedtime story, there is no actual use of made-up papal districts with naked emperors walking about.

Pitfall: Renaming project execution style to sound fancier

In the world of private equity, a venture is an investment with an extreme level of risk-taking. The most striking thing to know about ventures, is that due to the high risk, 9 out of 10 such undertakings will typically fail, in the sense that the money spent is lost. The investor only accept this extreme risk because when the odd star shoots, it goes far. But if not ready for 90% failure-count, don't go there. In some companies, there has been a shift to rename huge amounts of day-to-day projects into "ventures", or some other fashionable word of the day. The reason for doing this is mere vanity; the business side wants to strengthen their role as sponsors, and finds the word have an appetizing business flavor to it. One likely reason is that for some business managers, the mere word "project" leads the thoughts towards costly efforts without clear and immediate value. Maybe they associate with government wasting a heap of tax-payer's money on a politically correct activity, or some internal, logistically challenging but sales-wise mundane plan, like an office move. In contrast, what the business sponsor wants to order, is something with clout for profits, a "venture", and thanks to the change of words, the activities supposedly can have more focus on payoff and be run more professionally than if it was an ordinary project. This game with words is utterly futile, for two reasons:

First, project work is what it is under any name, and if some perspective on the organization's current project maturity contains unsatisfactory or unbalanced issues, just renaming the undertaking can never fix the real problem.

Second, the idea with a venture is risk-taking, and the mantra for a project is risk-control. Venture portfolios are supposed to withstand nine disappointing failures for one single success. Projects are supposedly planned to deliver on agreed goals on 100% of the projects. Which project office would actually accept a situation where 9 out of 10 projects close down without any of the intended results?

There should be an optimistic venture portfolio in an ambitious enterprise, but the initiatives there should be risky ventures, not projects in masquerade.

Pitfall: Too weak inter-style delimiting

In those organizations that naturally orient themselves around missions, the mission-level operating style naturally stands in between processes and projects. Many, if not most, corporations are heavily process-oriented due to their business model, and in those corporations, there is no mission-level at all.

This is the case in manufacturing industries such as a car factory, or process industries such as a refinery or a paper works plant. It is also the case in many administrative office workplaces that need process standardization at the heart of the business model, such as a bank. Finally, it is also a fact in most service facilities like supermarkets, salons, car repair shops, etc., etc.

Because there is no mission-level in these organization, the delimiting between process and project work is often too weak. Process managers are often the same persons as the project owners, the same personnel is allocated over and over and dragged back into the daily process whenever something happens (and it always does), and there is a slush of planned or intended tasks going back and forth between the processes and the projects. Project managers are then extremely frustrated of not having a proper delimitation towards the processes, finding the project resources busy with process tasks. Process managers are also disturbed by the projects, need to safeguard their processes, and can prefer to watch a project fail rather than see their daily processes suffer more.

Regular employees get caught in the crossfire and face the choice what to do. Most do a little of both, try to stay loyal until it simply becomes too much, then for a while focus only on the most urgent process tasks, and if the crossfire continues for too long, give up a deep sigh, down tools, call in sick, or resign.

Pitfall: Too strong inter-style delimiting

A corporation that has an unusually strong mission style level, will have a strong focus on synchronizing the line tasks with the missions and have an embedded change process for how updated data from process tasks are fed into the missions.

The missions have respect for the process, because the processes actually builds the mission. Without the tasks executed with precision on time, the mission will not take off, and even if it does, will have no chance to succeed. So the mission commanders are dependent of the process managers, and they therefore respect the roles each of them play for successful missions. But missionary operatives in the field are suspicious about projects, especially those that run at the headquarters. This is for two main reasons:

The first (and officially displayed) reason is because the mission level excel in their current standard operating procedure, and anything else is a risk of disturbance and even accidents.

The second reason for this suspicion against projects is that the role of project manager is typically not anywhere nearly as respected as the mission commanders are, in the mission oriented parts in the organization, and therefore the project managers can be ridiculed for their funny feathers and the complete lack of status from mission completions (the only thing that counts for a earnest field operative). Everything combined sets up an entrenched internal resistance from the corps of missionary operatives against the project teams. So, a project need to be very, very diplomatic in introducing carefully prepared and step-wise changes that are proven for the better, and allow the smoothest possible introduction of such changes into the standard operating procedures. Even with all these diplomatic skills, the project can hit a wall, where the delimitations between execution styles are blocking progress.

The way these types of organizations try to overcome this pitfall is of course to "borrow" personnel from the mission operatives into the most visible parts of the projects. In all projects it makes sense to have representatives from "users" so that all work is grounded in reality and tap into the tacit knowledge of long experience, so that the project can produce good and useful output. What I refer to as a visibility show is when senior operatives for symbolical figureheads in order to be politically accepted, and carefully appointed users are taken as symbolic hostage for project political reasons, i.e., not only for the mission-level operatives to contribute with knowledge in the project teams, but also be joint scapegoats if things turn around in a bad way.

We can suspect that this pitfall is present when the official project manager is a senior operative that primarily oversees the general direction of the project, act as a photo byline and just by being in display will help the project output to land well with the mission-level corps. Then there is of course some type of administrative project manager who does all the chores in the background and practically try to run the project in all aspects other than the political one. This setup can work, but also cripples the effectiveness of daily project management, and obscures the governance and steering principles, planting seeds for misdirected efforts or even spectacular project failures. So it is more advantageous - and in accordance to best practices of project management - to appoint senior mission operatives for the project steering committee, and assign the mission-level figurehead as the project owner to chair the steering committee.

9

Resources

The Third Strategic Question:
**Which distinct *capabilities*
are essential for the differentiation?**

On the resources axis, we enlist everything that is mustered or bought for use in any part of operations, and has the competence and capacity needed for the products.

The typical resources are employees, consultants, goods and services in procurement chains, partner contributions, and any additional suppliers input. The management structure for this, and all the employees, is often called the line organization. Typically, rents are paid monthly, names of rental payment can differ; salary, remuneration, leasing fee, etc. In the Glass Cube

Strategy, we can simulate as if all resources are being rented. If an asset, such as a building, is used as a resource, we reckon the funding cost for that asset as similar to rent.

Shareholder equity, loans, and other financing is used to fund acquisitions or pay rental costs of resources. So, in this sense, we regard the financing part of the balance sheet as an explanation to how resources were mobilized. The financing opportunities are important but is not supposed to overshadow the need of products and operations. A corporation that is putting too much focus on raising capital, may have trouble with its product and/or its operations, which will become quite obvious, sooner or later.

Corporate taxes paid are also listed on the resourcing side, as a cost for societal residency.

The earnings result when operating costs and taxes have been subtracted from the product revenues, we also list on the resourcing side, and in practice handle it as a cost for the ownership equity resourcing. By doing so, the resourcing side equals the product revenue side in monetary terms.

The basic accounting equation for the balance sheet shows how assets was funded by liabilities or shareholder equity, and although this is important for the cost structure and the control of the firm, there can be many variants of funding that may be equally acceptable in different situations, and dependent on the history of a particular firm and the ownership structure. Two different paths that lead to the present operation can have different sheets for historic reasons, and one does not has to be better than the other. The balance sheet is an important artifact in the Glass Cube Strategy because at every moment, it must be clear how the corporation is financed. Who are the real owners? How is management connected to owners? These facts are crucial for cross-checking that procurement is not corrupted into a sub-optimal sourcing that benefits one of the owners, or one of the managers. It can also give warnings of potentially corrupted compensation levels.

Type of value generated

The value generation along this axis is: the efficient line-up of competence, vendors, material, and equipment needed for the operations axis. Not only today, but also tomorrow and the day after tomorrow. Only

an engaged and forward-looking procurement planning will better the odds that resources will in fact
line-up correctly tomorrow when suddenly needed.
There can be costs today to ensure better line-up
tomorrow.

«»

Resources are not only material and labor used
in direct production; there is also the whole range of
complementary sourcing for activities like administration, bookkeeping, training, reparations, cleaning, and
so on. Depending on the nature of the business, inci-
dental expenses for complementary resources, or *faux
frais*, might add up to a considerable part of total costs.
These resources are deployed onto the Operations axis
and are allocated to the profit-loss sheets of Products
and Operations business units according to overhead
accounting rules. In an office operation, it is mainly administrative overhead , and in a factory there is also a
huge manufacturing overhead. It is completely normal
that the amount of overhead to be allocated becomes
greater than the direct cost of goods, which implies

that the overhead allocation method and calibrations is very important in business control.

Pitfall: No-one foots reservation costs

One consequence of slimmed organizations, is the sub-optimization that occurs when no profit/loss unit has any reason to foot reservation costs that could benefit the corporation as a whole.

Especially problematic is the human resources with a growing proportion of contingency workers, including contractors. As there may be long lead times for recruiting similar staff and even if same persons can in theory be asked to return, the emotional drawbacks of mismanaged relations, with lowered trust and loyalty, may simply reduce motivation and dilute possibilities to reengage. In practical terms, this means that after a line team is dismissed, for whatever reason, or when a project has come to a planned close, the corporation can loose good staff or consultants because they need to leave and seek other employment, and that departure can be permanent. Maybe both the corporation and the person wanted to prolong a relation, but the local unit had no immediate position to fill, and no compromise was imaginable on either side. However, in a wider outlook it can sometimes be the case that already the next day, or only a couple of weeks later, that very resource would be very useful elsewhere in a similar role, or the person would have enjoyed try that other role and do a good job at it, if given the chance. The sourcing at the second unit is not lucid at the first unit, and vice versa, due to internal opacity. Even if it was, there is often no mechanism to act on the information. From a corporate standpoint, it can be optimal to keep a particular resource enlisted for an imminent redeployment. Either the resource could do some minor backlog work while waiting for the new main assignment to start, or simply be on hold at some reduced rate for reservation cost previously negotiated. But that type of scheduling is typically not happening, so instead persons are dismissed, even while a similar unit starts resourcing to find someone else with a fairly similar profile. For the contingency workforce, lead times, transaction costs, and training costs, are not always properly evaluated against reservation costs.

A simple idea to partially avoid this pitfall could be this: a special procurement unit could be assigned a central role in short-term demand overview, bridge minor gaps, and pool internal fees into a reservation cost budget, and be evaluated for profit/loss as a resource management service.

Clearly, there will remain differences between how permanent employees are treated compared with temporary staff and contractors that make up the contingency workforce. But even with contractors, there can sometimes be tactical advantages of clever slotting for the ones that have been doing good recent work, instead of seeing them go sign up at a competitor never to return.

«»

With the concept of employment, there is a silent agreement that reservation costs are silent and expected in between tasks, missions, or projects. Regardless of contract type, any human resource about to roll-off an assignment, could be presented with the whole list of roles waiting to be filled in the near-term, and an opportunity to apply also for lateral but realistic moves.

Job rotation openings, with minimal formal complication and with mutual respect between resources and operations management, could be stimulating, educational, and immensely loyalty-building.

Pitfall: Thinning Threads

Task shifting problems are no longer only a headache for a few key persons, but for everyone, and as many missions, projects, and miscellaneous ambitions are started and running simultaneously, everyone finds themselves shredded into thinner and thinner threads, and that the time for task shifting becomes almost as much as the time for working.

An idea how to partially avoid this pitfall: recognize the task shifting time as a true cost, and work more on lining up projects and missions so that participants are in fewer tracks simultaneously. If a person is needed for project work, consider backfilling on operations tasks for that resource. Evaluate the ongoing need of backfills and have a realistic minimum level of slack and backups, to allow for missions and projects. Project office must share the pipeline with resourcing managers, and make sure that the company has a holistic cost perspective on manning both tasks, missions, and projects.

Pitfall: Disturbances Quick-Fix

After the last forty years of slowly maturing two-dimensional project-line matrices around the world, office workers of today typically find themselves having three categories of managers telling them what to do: the immediate line manager, the project managers, and the product managers. As if that is not enough, there is also a swarm of those managers' assistants, official aide-de-camps, unofficial helpers, and various opposing internal and external antagonists.

In this flow of information, lobbying, controlling, and more or less benevolent suggestions and requests, many line managers are mostly in the job of "shielding", i.e., trying to block access and give a few hours of protected time for their staffers to actually get somewhere with anything.

Sometimes, there are experiments with trying to institute a "non-interruptive day". The idea there is that one day each week, say Wednesdays or Fridays, all staff should let colleagues work on their respective assignments, and minimize contacts. It is not forbidden to talk to someone during a break, but to actively interrupt someone is to be avoided during that day. The champion promises that if everyone just holds their questions to the next day, then at least once a week, everyone gets a decent chance to get good traction on their own assignments. At first, this idea sounds worth trying, but the inherent problem is of course, that to get ahead with an assignment, one needs to ask and coordinate with colleagues. In some roles, it can be possible to work a whole day without a need to check anything with anyone, but in most roles it is practically impossible. Typically, after a staggering start when the "non-interruptive day" is proclaimed, it goes so-and-so for a couple of weeks: the timid and rule-oriented people try stick to the principle, and then it collapses and everything is as back before again, often without an official burial of the idea, it just silently disappears into the huge archive of tried things.

A suggestion to avoid this pitfall is to simply acknowledge that there is no quick fix on the disturbances challenges in the workplace, and that the only (partial) remedy is to constantly work on the organizational and team culture, to help each other find a balance between unnecessary disturbance, and necessary cooperation. If continuous disturbances are impacting the ability to focus, then operating procedures need to be improved, data sharing become more open, and documentation strengthened. To lock the doors does not make that need go away.

10

Shaping the Metaphor

In the previous chapters, we have kept the domains of products, operations, and resources as three closely interacting yet separate dimensions when understanding or managing a corporation.

Now, let us visually join them into place with each other. Verily, attaching three independent axes[70] at right angles to make a shape (with six equally sized faces), is of course resulting in a cube[71]. Moreover, to make things easy for starters, we can decide that each side of this cube has a fixed length of 100% of whatever top numeric value can be measured for the corporation

---

[70] Because these directions are at right angles to each other, it is possible to explore points along one axis, without having to simultaneously change coordinates on the other two axes.
[71] This glorious Platonic surface can also be appellated "regular hexahedron" because of its six square faces that meet each other at right angles. But the word "cube" is so much nicer and easier to say.

along that axis at that time, so the shape we begin to draw in this way is a "unit cube".

The interior of the cube consists of many shapes, some distinctly separated, some overlapping, and some inside others. Some of the interior shapes are *prisms* within the corporate Glass Cube. The analogy is that the biggest such prisms are organizational sub-entities typically named "divisions" or "business areas", i.e., sub-entities that are responsible for some of the products, part of operations, and some of the resources, i.e. they are coordinating along all three dimensions. Since business areas are almost never splitting up an enterprise cube in the exact same proportions along all three axes, that is why they become prisms, not subcubes. The prisms can be slanted and irregular, depending on how the control structures and decision cultures in a particular corporation have become. Divisions that are very independent, or even separate companies within a conglomerate, form prisms that are unusually distinct rectangular boxes, called cuboids.

Other shapes that can be illustrated within the Glass Cube, are two-dimensional rectangles that can be thought of as thin *sheets*, laying out coordination efforts along two of the enterprise axes, but not the third. A project-resource matrix is such a sheet.

«»

The surroundings for our cube is the whole of enterprise space. So, we can think of the apparent void around the cube to be the global pool of all other resources currently not available for the corporation to use in its own operations, the world's other simultaneous business activities going on all around that are not performed by this corporation, and all worldwide available products not delivered by it. Granted, there are some things in that vast enterprise space that are touching or are quite near this cube, because of joined delivery chains, active alliances and many other dependencies. Then there are many other things that are farther away, but still in the vicinity of operations, so to say. Nothing in enterprise space is theoretically completely irrelevant to a particular corporate cube (think about butterfly effects where small changes far away can make events pass a tipping point somewhere else), but in practice some things are indeed off by several degrees of separation, and can be simplified away from our observation and view.

«»

Now, let us for a moment also apply the dimension of time. Behind the surfaces of the cube, there is the three-dimensional snapshot of the current activities within the corporation. Obviously, events are not static and the representing cube is therefore constantly morphing internally. Most of the intra-cube changes that can be seen, are regular internal day-to-day fluctuations.

When animating these changes in spacetime[72], we can see this ongoing development and unfolding events (graphically, if sub-cube fractions are slightly colorized or refracting effects in the light, it may become quite a kaleidoscopic visual effect).

The fluctuations are often flowing in a certain rhythm as resources are being reassigned to other

---

[72] When moving one time unit ahead, we are creating a four-dimensional hypercube (sometimes called a tesseract). The standard tesseract in Euclidean 4-space is the convex hull of the points (±1, ±1, ±1, ±1). The first mention I have found on the concept of tesseract is in Hinton (1888), p.118.

parts of operations according to schedules and plans, and normal shifts in matrices as different projects and operations tasks are fulfilling different parts of product delivery chains. It can be seasonal rhythms, divestments and investments, industry trends, regulatory shifts, and business environment effects, that are mirrored in the intra-cube fluctuations.

But there are also more dramatic events, even threatening the existence of the corporation. If resources are drained and operations stutter to a halt, the cube can implode. That is bankruptcy.

«»

At first, it is challenging to orient oneself around a three-dimensional shape such as a virtual cube, to see it from different angles, especially with unfolding events ongoing. Haphazardly, we get conveniently stuck at a viewpoint, out of familiarity with our nearby area. Shifting our vantage point requires a deliberate effort, like when looking at those simple drawings of a cube and then flip one's mind between two possible angles of looking at the same drawing[73]. The reason an effort is required to change the view is that one has to overcome built-in cognitive shortcuts: how I first see an illustration of a three-dimensional cube drawn in two dimensions, depends on performance tweaks for image processing in my personal biological neural network. It would be very surprising if not similar cognitive shortcuts happens when we view or experience complex ongoing phenomena in an organization. Supposedly, how we regard current affairs, or even begin initiate a visual metaphor for an organization, is (at least) as prejudiced at first glance, as when first viewing a simple drawing of a cube.

《》

Surfaces of the cube are supposed to be clean. With this expression, I mean that there should be no doubt what is part of the corporation, and what is not. For example, resources either belong to (or is assigned for work at) the corporation, or not; there can be no discussion

---

[73] On several occasions, Wittgenstein (1953, 1978) uses drawings of a cube in philosophical investigations. A drawing of a glass cube can also be seen as an inverted open box, or as three boards put together in an angle.

if money on a bank account is corporate funds, or not. Further, a person is either an employee or not, a consultant is either contracted or not. It also means that either the corporation is undertaking a certain piece of work, or not. On the operations side, a project is running or is closed. In more detail: a milestone is hit or not, and decision points requires 'go' or 'no-go', there are no states of being in between options, as non-decisions are also decisions. A particular product is being researched or produced (normally with intentions to be delivered), or there is no such effort underway, a service is currently performed or it is not.

Clean product surface implies that when delivering to customers, one should make sure that the hand-off points are precise, and expectations well-managed.

If the interface between the corporation and its surroundings starts to become too diffuse, this can lead to trouble sooner or later. An unclean surface is displayed as impurity in the visual representation. Strange and dangerous holes on the cube, porous texture at the surfaces, unexpected bulbs clinging on either side, these are all very much unwanted. In geometric terms, the cube should be a closed and neatly bounded[74] part of enterprise space. Mathematicians call this property of a shape "compactness"[75]. Because the boundaries of the corporation should be well-defined, its representing shape should certainly be kept immaculate as a compact unit cube. We will return to the upkeeping of "compactness" in the last part of the book.

Compactness does not imply opacity: that surfaces are smooth does not necessarily make them stealthy. That the interior is closed together without irregularities, does not have to make the interior shapes darkened into obscurity. A compact object can also be translucent, combining those two properties in a fine way. This is the real beauty of a glass cube.

«»

---

[74] More formally, this is the Heine-Borel Theorem: "A subset of Rn is compact if, and only if, it is closed and bounded". See: planetmath.org/proofofheineboreltheorem

[75] During the 20th century, "*compactness*" became one of the most useful and important notions in mathematics, and still is. See Sundström (2010).

Now, because glass is being used as metaphoric material in this book, let us delve into the real material of glass for a brief moment! This material is so common today, that we forget to see what a unique substance it is. Uses like windows, mirrors, windscreens, microscopes, telescopes come to mind, amongst many others. But originally, the material was more crafted for its beauty than for its utility. In a book about the history of glass[76], we can follow how glass has changed the way we see ourselves and the world, and ponder over it:

> Glass is brittle, which is one of its weaknesses, but it is also enormously durable and flexible, and in the creative hands of an experienced and knowledgeable craftsman, it is almost infinitely malleable.

The history book then continues its musing by quoting an earlier observation about the substance:

> Glass can take any colour and, though possessing no texture in the ordinary sense of the word, any surface treatment. As for responsiveness to light and

---

[76] Macfarlane and Martin (2002).

shade, it has no serious competitor. It is capable of extreme finish and delicacy, is clean, durable and compact, and may be graduated almost imperceptibly from transparency through translucency to opacity, from perfect reflection through diffusion to the completely matte surface. There is, in fact, hardly any surface quality that it cannot assume. Yet at the same time it has a highly characteristic nature and in whatever manner we treat it or whatever surface we impose upon it, it still retains that unmistakable 'glassiness'.

Of course, I am a plain follower in this symbolism, not in any way pioneering using glass as a metaphor. Due to its quality of transparency, it has long been, and is increasingly, popular in political discourses, in modern architecture, and works of art[77].

«»

In analogy with how the real material of glass can be both beautiful and useful, and how we can look at glass objects from different angles, using ourselves as

---

[77] Jarosinski (2007).

camera re-positioning devices, and discussing what we discover about the shape in front of us, I believe that illustrating a corporation as a Glass Cube is useful because it makes it into something that can be discussed as an abstract entity, and reminds us that we need to shift vantage points to see all the refracting colors and how the prisms inside are really joined together at a particular point in time.

This amalgamated object is more complex than an overly simplified drawing of a tree hierarchy "organigram", and therefore the cube is much better as a model of a real enterprise.

As the mathematician Charles Hinton stated 1885: as conscious minds, we best realize the oneness of past and future in open communication with each other, and with this effort corruption and evil will fall:

> Truth is nothing but an aspiration to our higher being. And the first sign of love towards individuals, as towards the world as distinguished from the easy and yielding good nature which always tries to please that which is nearest at the moment - is veracity.

This is the secret of the mysterious effect of science on our emotions - the simple description of fact, apart from our own conditions and prejudices.

And also in the material world around us, this is the secret of the beauty of the crystal and of still water.

For in them the near and the far are brought together; in their translucency they give an emblem of the one vision wherein a higher being grasps every part of the solid matter, of which we can only see outside and surface.

From *Scientific Romances*, by Charles H. Hinton[78]

---

[78] Hinton (1885).

Part III
GLASS CUBE
STRATEGY

11

Enlight with Integrity

The formulation of the Glass Cube Strategy is all about enlightenment with good intentions while respecting oneself as well as all what is protected. The formulation theme is therefore called "Enlight with Integrity".

Enlightening brings clarity. A brand can be loaded with mystery, if that is suitable for the type of product and its target customers: a perfume brand would be next to nothing without some allure. But the formal organization, and its legal and factual situation, is not allowed to have mysterious webs surrounding it. While brand can be exciting, the corporation must be crystal clear.

Translucency is not to be confused with nakedness, and it absolutely does not mean being without a spine when in contact with stakeholders: a strong stance on integrity and a defense of privacy when appropriate, is the twin companion to the clarity on everything else.

A company that has a culture of integrity will become significantly more profitable than others. Luigi Zingales at the University of Chicago analyzed one thousand companies and found that those with a culture of keeping their word, were rewarded for it[79].

The positive impact of a culture of integrity are not only related to a more constructive customer relation, but also to first- and second-order effects internally. This was brilliantly described thus:

> Perhaps the most important, but also most concealed, benefit is that integrity forces individuals and companies to invent. When we commit to confronting reality head-on, we close the door to managing impressions. Rather than looking like we are achieving results, we are left with no choice but to really achieve them.(...) Waffling on integrity almost always involves some element of avoidance. The problem is that too much of our attention goes to managing appearances and putting out fires, and too little to the actual work. Conversely, when you

---

[79] Guiso, L., Sapienza, P., and Zingales, L., (2013)

make a clear commitment to integrity, you face your mistakes and your limits, and you step up to the sorts of honest challenges that galvanize employees and senior leaders alike. Yes, this will mean making sacrifices. Initially, the results are likely to look worse, simply because you are telling more of the truth. Yet, as in the quality movement, the single biggest barrier to improvement may be overcoming assumptions about what is possible. Over time, you will propel your results to a level where others ask how you can afford to do it. And your answer? "Actually, contrary to popular belief, we have found that integrity is free."

Elizabeth Doty, network fellow of Harvard University's Edmond J. Safra Center for Ethics.[80]

So, everything that is inside the Glass Cube (i.e., pertinent facts about Products, Operations, Resources), that is formulating the current business of a corporation, will be publicly visible, on a passably summary level.

In few cases, a particularly unique product formula can be held confidential for competitive reasons, only disclosed for regulatory inspectors etc., but that

---

[80] Doty (2014)

level of secrecy is very exceptional. In all cases, the corporation will defend the basic privacy of its work-force, suppliers, and clients, as far as the defense is legally appropriate.

Principle 1: Open Product Content

Comparability is a major problem for buyers. Let us look at air travel booking, as an example. There are now plenty of websites helping the air traveler of today in finding tickets from various airlines, via possible routes to the destination, but the data provided by the industry for comparability is still surprisingly thin. At first glance, the listings may all seem like fully comparable commodities, when in fact, they are not. Different airlines and all the ticket classes and types involved, means that there are differences in baggage allowance, overweight charges, service levels, frequent-flyer points, re-booking conditions, etc. As of May 2015, these facts are still not part of comparisons. Trying to tabulate the differences and calculate a weighted comparison prices for the route including the conditions, simply would take too much effort for the consumer[81], hence the infamous low-cost airline "race to the bottom" when it comes to unbundling fares, and then performing fee additions.

If the industry is unwilling to streamline a common data format for other relevant trip info but just the departure and arrival time, and the base price - whatever that means, then the major booking websites should take hold of the comparison problem, and provide more intelligent comparisons for the individual consumer, where baggage allowance and payment processing fees and such things are all taken into consideration, to extent that these "add-ons" will be required at a later stage in the booking process or while traveling.

《》

Leaving airline-traveling, and looking at techniques for payment processing, it can be worth reiterating that the use of blockchain technology in bitcoins met with rising interest because it made its ledger public, although encrypted. In other words, the transac-

---

[81] The gaps in the air travel sales channel's data model is discussed in Coughlan (2013).

tion database is not kept in one central place, but instead circulated around to the users. That was surprisingly divergent from classic handling where the full control of the payment ledger is a core fundament, and only by being centralized can be entrusted. Distributing a core part of an infrastructure in this fashion makes it internet-style expandable[82], but the lack of central authority also makes it easy to get away with thefts, big and small, many such events have already happened already with bitcoins, and some quite suspicious troubles have taken place at bitcoin service providers, emptying the wallets of thousands of anonymous owners. So the problem with the bitcoin initiative was not in the ledger technology, but in basic trust. The obscurity on the background and operations is still extraordinary. Where the internet in itself has the ICANN institute as a common point for infrastructure governance dialogue, the bitcoin network has nothing. How many bitcoins are hedged by the anonymous founder, or have been already stolen? If a person

---

[82] Also, the distribution of the ledger imposes an accumulative footprint onto clients, making the technique relatively complicated for micro-transactions on portable devices. But with a layered approach, with aggregators, blockchain technology can likely be engineered in layers to create smaller footprints and achieve performance optimization in the periphery.

would not leave cash on the city sidewalk and expect it to remain there one week later, how come the same person leave bitcoins on a distant computer? It can only be because it felt to that person more like having a deposit on an electronic bank account, when it was definitely not so. As mentioned previously, the irreversibility and untraceability aspects of bitcoins promote criminal actions. So, lack of transparency can be a problem for legitimate users.

Our takeaway for the moment is that a sensitive part of a product, service, or infrastructure, that intuitively feel like proprietary core setup, can sometimes be distributed in surprising ways, if that is engineered as a designed feature. But also that while Open Product Content can include unusual or provocative setups, it may also need some complementary regulatory means of traceability to upkeep high enough levels of trust.

Principle 2: Open Product Pricing

The reason transparent prices is so extremely important in the market economy, is that it enables decentralized decisions. This in turn makes possible somewhat efficient allocation of goods and services in society, avoiding the even more terrible waste that could happen otherwise. Economy subject researchers take into consideration also the additional costs for searching, branding and advertising in a free competitive market, and still find that in general, the more price transparency, the better for consumers. These findings hold also when buying complicated products and services, and in business-to-business transactions when procuring complex products[83].

Traditionally, the focus of price information has been the availability of localized standard price lists, so that potential customers can make their basic comparisons between competing similar offers before buying from a distributor.

Over the last two decades, many comparison services has flourished online, where vendor websites are harvested for data, and the results conveniently presented to the researching customer, sorted for lowest price, or according to some factor weighting function calculating "best" option. Complementing the price data, there is typically some feedback ranking gathered

---

[83] See Austin and Gravelle (2008) considering evidence of price transparency, with a focus on health markets.

somehow from previous customers (showed as stars or points) that gives some additional flavor to the sorted price list.

It is still unusual that producers and distributors present to potential customers how they have set their prices, i.e., disclosing the price function, if not completely, then at least for all the factors that the customer can influence by revising the request slightly. To reach some understanding of the price function, the researching customer typically need to collect several quotes from the vendor and try to roughly reverse engineer the price function, or at least experimentally study the effect of changing a delivery date or some of the product content.

«»

Many manufacturers use software called Configure Price Quote (CPQ) to take manual work out of quotation preparation. It is not certain that customer receives more insight thanks to digital configurators, but it opens up for such possibilities.

One early example of user-friendly online configuration tools for customers, was the "build-your-car" applications that started to appear on automobile global brand websites around 1998, combining the joy of selecting add-ons and options, with clear price information[84].

Very seldom, the customer is allowed to see if and exactly how the vendor charge differently to different customers or groups. Everyone knows that price discrimination is part of business, but exactly how and when, is surprisingly secretive. I assume that this secrecy is not only for competitive reasons, but also in an attempt to avoid a risk that retail consumers feel short-changed somehow. The latter reason should

---

[84] I recall from working with the global portal for a car brand back in 1999, the enthusiasm for a build-your-car app, how it let customers configure their favorite virtual car online before visiting a retailer (and also review published detailed price sheets online), how this new app also opened up for more build-on-order manufacturing , and an improved customer purchase experience. But that there were some initial concerns that this new ease of finding detailed prices also for neighboring countries could affect some buyers, perhaps leading some of them to make a trip and buy their car from a foreign dealer and arrange with importing it, if that would net them a better deal, instead of buying the same car through a local dealer. Earlier, few customers went about collecting brochures from neighbor countries, so targeted distribution of printed price sheets into local markets was arguably more controlled by the marketing function before price lists became published on the web. This hesitation and fearing the "information leakage" and its unforeseen possible changes in consumer behavior, is very typical when increasing price transparency.

gradually diminish over time, as consumers everywhere get more and more accustomed to pricing factors and the role of distribution costs[85].

As the inter-firm transactions costs continue reducing thanks to digital contracting channels, public procurement transparency increase worldwide, and price comparison portals develop and their scope get wider and wider, I think that paternalistic price discrimination secrecy will gradually diminish both on consumer markets and also in business to business relations, and real-time price transparency on products and services will become surprisingly high.

Principle 3: Open Product Roadmap

A factor with paramount impact on the organization's future, is how product management interplays with

---

[85] Personally, I completely accept the fact that when buying four rolls of toilet paper in a grocery store, these commodity items will cost more apiece than if I was an officer in a regional council buying the very same product for, say, four major hospitals. Imagine eight full-size containers in one single order, to be sent by trucks directly from a factory, and how that changes the distribution and selling cost structure dramatically. I would be appalled if the regional council paid the same price per item that I paid in a grocery store.

the resources-projects matrix, week by week and year by year. In this interplay, there should be an intense communication on product vision, and the wider goals that unite the teams. To achieve this, the risk assessments and the road maps have to be vivid and compelling, not only in a once-off workshop in one project, but incessantly and cross-projects, and the ongoing prioritizations at the project portfolio level must be lightened up for transparency. The more that staff and customers share a mutual understanding on the bigger picture of where the organization is heading with all efforts, the more the chance of success. As the use of scenario planning has increased over the last decades, business teams become better at shifting the emphasis of discussion from just the present situation, to a shared understanding of where to better arrive in the future[86].

The expression "creating the market" is an illustrative shorthand for certain risk-taking activities[87] in business development, that can pay off well, but I rec-

---

[86] Rigby and Bilodeau (2007) found that in faster-changing environment, scenario and contingency planning does increase.

[87] What the slogan "create the market" wants to convey is that the company is proactively exploring a hitherto unserviced market segment, preparing an offering that is hopefully among the first to launch into that embryonic segment.

ommend that the expression is used with some care. Industries can indeed be reshaped and new market segments open up, by creative recombination and clever marketing. The corporation owns its product offerings, and can detect and identify new opportunities, but (unless in monopoly or extreme corruption) it never "owns" the market and can therefore hardly by resources "create" a market, if there is no factual (albeit dormant) interest there to meet and serve. Admittedly, it is still an inspirational motto for certain risky initiatives.

Product strategy and road maps are all about looking through the front windscreen, not trying to drive a car full speed ahead by staring into the rear-view mirrors. Other success factors of business, like financing and resourcing can be top-notch, but without motivational and sound direction along the product axis, and buy-in from customers and employees on the product roadmap, the enterprise inevitably begins to wobble, and finally fails.

Principle 4: Open Operations Status

The most visually striking, and data-rich part of the implementation of Glass Cube Strategy, is the artifacts, feeds, and displays generated according to the principle of *Open Operations Status*. This principle is in essence about adopting an open data attitude on many aspects of the ongoing operations, and especially the parts that interface with customers. If a data stream is not restricted, it can by default be opened, at first for internal use, and if not classified as sensitive, also for external view. All internal data is normally accessible for those who can use it for something, even if only for learning.

Employees will have access to rich "Dashboard für Alles" portals with comprehensive insight on ongoing workflows, missions, and all non-secret projects. The general public will see in real-time how missions unfold, whether they are customers for that mission or not. Projects will share certain milestone information with other adjacent projects, internally and externally, on their progress and concerns, as long as the sharing costs to the project, or the sensitivity of the information, is not hindering such cross-project advise.

Sometimes, 3rd parties will use publicly available data streams, re-package the information, and display the facts in a new way, a way that the corporation will find useful and pay a fee to utilize in that format. A striking example of an unexpected 3rd party provider, that I believe is quite typical of what will follow in all industries and sectors, is the website flightradar24.com that is showing worldwide flights in progress[88]. As opposed to a similar service, FlightAware, the website flightradar24 had no business connection with aviation technology firms, yet could achieve tremendous data quality thanks to "crowd-sourcing". A small but important note on privacy concerns, is that the site upkeeps a global blocking list, and permanently refrain from displaying anything of certain airplanes after request from owners or operators. Whatever happens in the future with flightradar24 as a business, the knockout of

---

[88] The website flightrader24 started as a hobby project in 2006 when a couple of aviation geeks decided to graphically display data received from transmitters on planes in Northern Europe. Contrary to the name of the website, it has nothing to do with radar, as it is using positioning code from Automatic Dependent Surveillance-Broadcast (ADS-B) transmitters, devices that are sending positioning data from airplanes. Anyone with a purposedly set up receiver can pick up and interpret those radio signals. In 2009, flightradar24 opened up its data feed for associated enthusiasts to upload data from their receivers. In less than six months, the whole of Europe was covered. Most parts of the world followed, and the

the whole story is that the website was not set up by an expensive cross-industry project, neither was it a government statistics website, but the practical result of a focused effort of collecting and using publicly available signals, and present the realtime situation for easy view.

«»

Reiterating the point about team competence and responsibilities: adopting the *Open Operations Status* principle must not cripple the operations team in doing their daily work.

Status display is not meant to be a "big brother" camera recording every move. It is up to the team to negotiate with managers and business controllers what the appropriate operational monitoring points can be, and how it helps the operations organization towards better efficiency and the corporation towards goals of Glass Cube Strategy building trust with stakeholders

----

progress of thousands of flights can now be followed in realtime on a map. Even aircraft that only carry the legacy "Mode S" transponders can be positioned, using a form of triangulation. Oceanic coverage is still lacking, but will surely be introduced, one way or the other, perhaps by putting receivers on merchant ships traveling the seas. See Croft(2015).

through an appropriate and appreciated level of transparency into operations.

«»

Being a vital piece of the strategy on trustworthiness, the choice of vocabulary in operations is important for clarity and relevance, and euphemisms should be avoided.

A business strategy book can delve in metaphors and analogies that helps seeing and understanding the invisible aspects of organization, but for Open Operations Status, all common actions and objects in the real world should keep their most common and least ambiguous names, with a speak-the-truth and no-nonsense approach.

To make a dramatic example about unwanted euphemisms: something is unsettlingly wrong when military personnel watch a computer display as if it is a game, and use terminology from sports or entertainment, even for the most caustic situations any employee could face in any vocation: shouting "touchdown", "score", or "jackpot" when a symbol on the display disappears on a monitor after weapon fire. The relatives of the dead can sometimes come about to later watch video recordings of the event, with such language included. These are not only isolated, adolescent immaturities, but also questions whether supervising officers are not taking their responsibilities entirely serious. If real people just died, it was a kill, not a "jackpot". The more civilians and children who died, the more disgusting the choice of words. Some nations and military groups seem to have more problems with tasteless expressions than others. Probably, the background to this type of language has to do with anxiety.

Another side of the same coin, is an exaggerated use of invented acronyms, instead of simple and already available words. Often, a short combination of two simple words could be used to describe a device or phenomenon, instead of a five-letter acronym of long and complicated words. The multitude of technical expressions combined with jargon, artificially builds a sense of professionalism, by establishing an internal vocabulary that is hard to penetrate for the outsider. The acronym feast is a well-known phenomenon in military and in engineering, but also in medicine, psychology, and management. Probably, the factor causing most of the unnecessary acronyms is a pretense to professional superiority.

In business in general, and in the strive towards *Open Operations Status,* my advice is to make a deliberate effort to resist jargon, speak plainly, and don't fall into word games. If an indicator on a status display is about some of the negative aspects of operations, such as delays, queues, customer complaints or defective parts, don't cover up. Use common and normal words. Things are what they are.

Principle 5: Open Operations Archives

Defaulting to transparency is equally impelling for historical data, no matter if it relates to last week or last year. Key elements from Open Operations Status builds up an archive of information. To have these available to all staff, or in many cases to the general public, is of course uneasy in the beginning. As provocative it can be in the beginning, as addictive it becomes. Examples of information available in the Open Operations Archives are:

- Equity breakdown every shareholder
- Monthly income statement and expense sheets

- Actual salaries for all current line positions
- Compensations to consultants
- Open line positions and their salaries
- Product balance sheets
- Product revenue sheets
- Procured material and services
- Delivery statistics
- Allocation statistics

Some data points need to be anonymized, if a supplier or customer refuse that their pricing be disclosed. This can be solved by having undisclosed rows on the product revenue sheets. If some information about the workforce would trespass individual privacy, it must also be aggregated into a level where it no longer poses a privacy problem. We will get back to that side of the coin as Principle 8 below.

Data in Operations Archives has at least three levels: Confidential, Internal, and Public. The way to look at the principle of *Open Operations Archives* is that business data should be open (Internal or Public) unless explicitly classified as Confidential, for very good reason. That is the meaning of defaulting to transparency.

Correspondence archives

Although e-mail is the current channel with highest traffic in corporate messaging, it may have passed its peak and will reduce in volume as more and more coordination and information sharing will take place on digital dashboards and various portals.

A message can just as well be a comment on a digital object in a workflow portal that is within the team, or cross-organizational.

The traditional way of handling e-mail in the two first decades of intensive and widespread use, i.e., between circa 1995 and 2015, have been in unstabilized mixes of need-to-know dialogues that expanded and threaded into side-tracks where subject lines lost their meaning, and for various broadcasts. For many officers, it became a struggle to avoid choking each others inboxes, while asking for and spreading information around the organization. *De facto* usage policies took long time to establish, and are still wobbling in many places.

The two main reasons of putting someone on the "cc:" row when drafting an email in the office were:

1) when you remembered that someone might benefit to know, and the primary addressee will not mind the copying.

2) when you pulled in that cc inclusion as a micro-insurance, just in case that may save your back later when something goes wrong. By including others in the information flow, many people felt a reduced fear of personal responsibility, even if it was not realistic, or even appropriate, that a manager (or whoever that extra person was for the extra copy) should actually jump into the thread with endorsements or guidance, or react in any other way in the general traffic noise.

Sometimes, the culture and policies around practical e-mail use have been swinging back and forth, not only within an organization, but also individually, depending on current stress level and even mood. I believe some of the additional noise came from a lack of good archiving policy. Then to reduce the noise, we skip people that does not need to know urgently, or that will need to know, but only in the future. It was only polite not to disturb people unnecessarily, and a matter of tact.

Similar arguments came on the swings on using the "reply all" function, to reduce overall noise; replying only to sender of the last statement is more discreet, and can cut off branches that will otherwise keep disturbing too many colleagues. However, there may be situations when this pruning leaves questions unanswered in future searches. To shift through old emails and stumble upon one's own question again, still hanging in the air unanswered, was not helping much.

Although important standard operating procedures in a corporation shall be recorded in other forms than e-mails, in reality there is also indispensable background and many special cases that have been reviewed and managed somewhere in a previous dialogue, which is quickly lost, or practically lost by being dislocated too far away from the person who could benefit knowing about it later. Messages had to be repeated, re-requested, or awaited, if someone was new, out-of-office, or for all other reasons. Even if the same person was still in charge of the task later, it could have been deleted for quota reasons. The mere opacity of the exaggeratedly separated channels, was the main problem. To request a copy of an old message would require knowledge of the original, which was illogical for the most parts. It would also require time from the original author to retrieve and send a copy. So the tra-

ditional way to find out about things, was that someone closer to the enquirer had partial knowledge and
responded with clues and pointers onwards, contribut-
ing to more noise. To not disturb people about past issues, the original knowledge was sometimes not included at all in the task, which started anew,
sometimes many times with different people at different places.

When a person was out of office, or that person
had retired or resigned, or ran out of email disk quota
and deleted the personal archives, most of the previous
correspondence involving that person was for all practical aspects lost forever, especially if concerned a two-
party communication with an external counterparty,
and thus no other remaining member of the thread
was still around.

In general, I would say that the whole handling
surrounding e-mail during its first circa twenty years
of widespread use in business, was more similar to
fleeting and disparate telephone calls than to a secured
flow of pieces of intellectual capital, supposed to be
valued and that can help constitute the current state of
affairs and provide ample background when later
needed. It was as if most officers were of the common

opinion that as telephone calls were normally not recorded, then e-mail correspondence should not be saved for other people to look at later, except in very special cases.

Only gradually, functions began to set up shared inboxes for workflows where it was obvious that personal inboxes were inappropriate or unpractical.

Having distribution lists for emails, are still the widespread shorthand for putting certain employees on the "cc" row in broadcasts. There are three drawbacks with the common technique of such internal distribution lists. The first is that it multiplies copies and puts the filtering burden on the recipients, often staff with heavy email volumes. The second is that it is a distribution to the current members of the list. Future members will typically not have the full history available. The third drawback is that distribution lists, by their multiplication effect need to keep their relevance and minimize traffic. It is hardly socially acceptable, perhaps even harakiri, to send ones latest wild idea to a management distribution list. To avoid over-use and choking, some distribution lists (example: 'AllEmployees') have been locked-down in many organizations, so that only certain people can send to these lists. Altogether, I believe distribution lists may have been a handy feature in email clients for a period, but has been superseded by better alternatives, and can be put to rest very soon.

Shared inboxes are another matter, since they represent a virtual recipient that is supposed to read and take action on a message. Some departments at some organizations are already very accustomed to shared inboxes, e.g. at backoffice operations in financial firms, where the correspondence with counterparties via functional inboxes have been essential in the workflows. As specialized workflow platforms have been introduced in several areas, the traffic between functional emails is slowly reducing. But for queries that do not naturally reside on a workflow platform, the functional recipient is still the best route. Sometimes these emails have business significance, and it would nowadays be an unprofessional touch to have them going between personal addressees only, without involving the functional inbox. For backoffice operations at banks, the concept of shared inboxes for external contacts incoming, is quite natural. Probably, those inboxes were introduced in parallel with replacement of the department fax machines, so nothing surprising in the concept, just a better solution. Also, in first-line support and helpdesk teams in customer services departments, the shared functional inbox is a centerpiece in day-to-day incoming requests management, call dispatch, and general workflow.

The difference between a functional shared inbox and a transparent designated email archive, is that the shared inbox is for a specific team to monitor and act upon, according to team dispatch and team workflow, whereas a transparent email archive is searchable and readable for (typically) anyone in the organization (and in some situations for external parties with appropriate credentials to that archive).

Although the shared inbox have sometimes been put not only as a primary addressee, but also by an internal author, on "cc" row when originating an outgoing communication, as a way to inform other team members about the topic, the original use for the shared inbox is to be a point of contact, ie for others to put on the "to" row. My recommendation is that internal authors discontinue setting their functional inbox "cc", and use the specially-designated team archive to receive correspondence copies or information snippets that are not in the core workflow for functional inbox management.

A helpdesk team have a functional shared inbox that customers can send questions to. Then there should be another archive where staff and customers alike can look for solutions and answers to previous questions. The archive can have different layers, like internal only thread, archive with trace records for a particular customer only, archive on issues viewable to current customers only, or a part of the archive for general public access to frequently asked questions. This type of support archive can be an amalgamation of emails, workflow data and references, and additional case notes.

In other workplaces, there are still only the personal inboxes and no precise policy for message archiving from a corporate knowledge management perspective. Typically, a new person in a team then has a hard time to catch up with previous work and and already discussed topics, since most of the previous electronic conversations were only in personal email threads, chats, and other miscellaneous channels without any overarching idea on general tracing and captures for the future. Poor rookies then had to ask again and again about what has been done, and how it was done. These rewinds and repeats involved a lot of email forwarding, and reiterating the past which was mostly boring for the regular staffers. Helpful persons will always be needed to guide and introduce, and everyone is more interesting in looking forward and doing new things. But no organization is completely without history, a trace that is important to revisit in order to proceed correctly onwards, and it was in many places unnecessarily time consuming to learn details about the recent past. If it takes a year of introductions and hundreds of questions, for a rookie to graduate to become a useful operational resource, that is clearly wrong. Admittedly, an amount of time for hands-on practicing to become more skilled, before starting on real delivery work is indispensable, to safeguard a minimally acceptable quality level. Lengthy introduction periods can be a warning that plenty of time is lost in the friction of trying to collect information already in the work-group's joint knowledge base but hard to reach.

With portals running domain-specific platforms for business data management, the situation is improving, so that core workflow matters are collected into the relevant workflow application, where it can be reviewed later as needed. But correspondence more on discussion-level, and on all the slightly more general topics than the standard cases captured into specialized applications, are often disregarded, and therefore sidetracked for shredding. Moving communication flows into specialized portals must not imply that there is no longer any archive.

The default option in mail clients should be "opt-out archiving" where a copy of incoming and outgoing messages on an issue is suggested to be filed into the most relevant function/project archive.

This does not mean that corporate servers are to snatch and copy every message written, *en masse*. To perform involuntary and automated copying for widespread display will be counterproductive, because that risks pushing communication into other channels. The concept of "opt-out archiving" is a systematic voluntary archiving, without unknown secret caches.

«»

Default to transparency means that you and your colleagues can later access information when you want to. If increased openness suddenly makes irrelevant things starting to be pushed in your face[89], then the whole point of transparency in business was misunderstood. Your inboxes are not to be swamped with copies causing an information overload, yet there are to be rich and ample traces in the archives for possible research and revisit whenever needed. It also means that you remain in reasonable control of visibility of what you write for work.

Archived conversations, no matter if they are a month or a year old, deserve polite civil inattention - that unobtrusive and peaceful scanning - so as to allow for neutral interaction.

In other words, feel free to read archives to find background to the current situation, but show tact when commenting the topic of conversation afterwards. The longer time that passed, the more discretion is needed with any post-facto opinions.

Principle 6: Open Books

To continue from the spotlight visited in chapter 3 on "open-book accounting", we will now expand that concept into a strategic principle. The additional back-

---

[89] Well put by Lee (2014).

ground for doing so, is the continuously increasing pressure and expectations from external and internal stakeholders, as well as regulators, on more transparent financial reporting, and with ever shorter delay.

The reasonable consequence of shorter reporting cycles, leading towards a new norm of high-frequency financial reporting, is that the current obsession on annual and quarterly reports will diminish. I would not say that annual checkpoints will totally vanish, because for practical reasons, tax filing and other checkpoints will keep on to monthly or annual cycles for the foreseeable future. However, most tax payments around the world will, one by one, be moved from annual to monthly cycles, with the annual report becoming a summary of preliminary tax payments during the year, and to make a final close. I believe that most types of taxes worldwide will come to have monthly filing and payment (e.g., VAT, and employer fees on wages), while a few types will keep on to annual final close (corporate income) for many years still.

Perhaps apart from national income tax purposes, most other stakeholders, and most statutory reporting, will have increasingly more aggressive expectations of shorter reporting cycles. This will put pressure on the finance departments in all corporations to install and configure accounting systems to use daily mark-to-market valuations whenever possible, streams for real-time entry of revised judgments, and fully automated accrual calculations and bookings[90].

«»

Beyond statutory financial reporting, business controllers are fully occupied with internal stakeholders and managers, designing and providing performance indicators. The emphasis on producing   qualitative indicators for situational awareness and as decision support, are enclosed both in the Open Operations Status principle, and in the Open Books principle. Many indicators are part of, or close to, the regulatory accounting books, for example:

- Indicators primarily in the Products dimension (financial value of assets and goodwill investments, product balance sheets, product sales income, product direct costs, with periodizations and net present value estimations).

---

[90] See Wagenhofer (2007)

- Indicators primarily in the Operations dimension (activity-based costing, the expenses sheet pivoted by function, mission, or project).

- Indicators primarily in the Resources dimension (balance sheet items and notes on resources, available supplies, indicators on costs for procurement readiness and for contingent workforce)

- In addition, some advanced indicators can also be defined to describe matrix properties on different time horizons for the capacity sheets, the allocations sheets, and the delivery sheets.

Reporting activities that are not associated to mandatory reporting, requirements or to performance indicators on select operational or strategic parameters, can be eliminated. Remaining activities must be streamlined and standardized, and manual corrections minimized. Automated data streams technologies must be leveraged together with configured templates for near real-time throughput of calculated values into the indicator dashboards. Failing investments in high-quality content input streams into data warehouses and in so-called "smarter close" procedures,   business control and finance functions will have no chance to succeed in the barrage of new requests and overall increased expectations, without compromising accuracy[91].

«»

The model and the principle of *Open Books* can, and should, be expanded to include true value estimation of particularly relevant externalities.

All corporations create value for society (positive externalities) that are not shown in the accounting records, and also cause more or less cost to its surroundings that are not listed as costs (negative externalities).

In the short term, externalities have no immediate impact on the corporation's formal book-keeping, but as transparency increases and corporations spend more effort on mitigating negative externalities, and could become more appraised for its positive externalities, it is only reasonable to formalize, track, and show best estimations on main externalities, as part of the *Open Books* principle.

---

[91] Good advice can be found in pwc(2010)

The honesty displayed in including externalities in the reporting section will, for most stakeholders and for the general public, surely be more impressive than only having the bare-minimum honesty that is absolutely required for the legal accounting sections.

Principle 7: Open Resourcing

Corporate strategy is manifest in the iterations of resource allocation[92], rather than in any formal statements of "*the* strategy".

Whereas the principle of *Open Pricing* is about being transparent towards customers on product pricing functions, *Open Resourcing* is on being transparent to all stakeholders on the sourcing of capital, goods, services, and not least on remuneration data for the complete workforce (regardless if a person is employed or subcontractor). Implementing *Open Resourcing* implies at least three practical changes for future businesses, compared with today.

The first, and least controversial practical part, is the disclosing of procurement details, according to best practices for anti-corruption work, and put pres-

---

[92] Noda and Bower (1996)

sure upstream and downstream for the same. This will put ample light on the supply chain, increasing efforts that providers, and their sub-providers in turn, are legal entities of good standing, and that there is an ethical conduct during the decision process. Sellers are actually often quite used to these types of procedures in public procurement processes, so to step-wise introduce that type of post-selection disclosure on a voluntary basis within the private sector as a joint anti-corruption measurement between understanding enterprises, is not as problematic as one may first believe, and if big buyers introduce it, chain reaction proceed upstream through supply chains.

«»

The second part of *Open Resourcing* is that the entire workforce can bid for roles in the operations organization. The long-term resourcing is distinctly separated from the short-term operational allocations. Having a home base and line title, as an employee or subcontractor, is fundamentally separated from the active roles in a process team, a mission, or a project. Typically, one person has several roles simultaneously within the operations organization and also pending bids for upcoming roles. By allocation into multiple roles, more of a persons total competence can be put to use. Obviously, there is no point bidding for a role where one has not the stated necessary qualification of certification. When qualification can be possible via course work and role rotation trainee or other pre-qualifying effort, relevant competence packages are sometimes open for application, according to Human Resource policy and employment terms.   Human Resources is the corporate function having overall responsibility of the workforce bidding and role assignment process into the entire operations organization. Clearly, for a decent-size corporation the administrative effort of *Open Resourcing* would not be possible without an advanced and appropriate digital portal for the HR workflow.

For the individual, bidding is more proactive than being commanded, and the end results of a bidding process are better understanding and more motivation. *Open resourcing* is not injecting less guarantee into the contractual terms of the line title, it is only making the operational allocation decision process more transparent. At every moment the blend of employees and subcontractors is calibrated according to HR policy, procurement policy, contractual terms, and individual preferences. Individual movement between contracted staff and contingency workforce is completely undramatic, and goes in both directions.

«»

The slightly more controversial part of *Open Resourcing,* is letting employment terms (as well as consulting contracts terms) become more visible. For a contractor it is normally not a problem to compare work orders against remuneration levels that similar contractors are receiving for similar services, but for employees it can be strange and uncomfortable at first. There is still a wide-spread and irrational fear of becoming transparent on human resources, letting colleagues know about peer remunerations data across the board. But psychology teaches us differently: neuroscientists proclaim that our minds work best when not in "threat response mode", a mode wasting energy on covering up, investigating, and being upset about unfairness[93].

[93] Smith and Tabibnia (2012)

The initial reaction, that it would hurt employees too much if managers begin being truthful with relevant facts about compensation levels, and real feedback about a report's current possibilities to develop professionally and grow a career with the employer, may be completely missing the point[94]. Is it more correct to hand out annual white lies to an employee? What about the feeling of being set up? Will that not hurt more?

Another reaction is that publicized information about peer compensation would be used to press salaries down, via coercive force. From what can be seen in real-life situations, the effect seems to be opposite; it means negotiation fuel when both sides have more information, and strong negotiators immediately benefit from having more information entering the negotiation. When US corporations were forced to begin disclose executive pay to a higher degree, it did not seem to cause enough public pressure to cool off the executive compensation in the following years, which saw accelerated increases of payments. Enhanced disclosure on peer CEO payment may even have been a catalyst in the rapid rise. At least, the possible mitiga-

[94] Smith and Tabibnia (2012)

tion effect was overpowered by other factors affecting governance and compensation practices during the first years after the increased disclosure policy came into force[95]. The inequality between executive compensation and worker salaries in big companies have become hyperbolic, but if that gap is to be reduced, it will not be through returning to a business world of more secrecy behind closed doors.

«»

Supply chains are certainly not only about raw material such as metal, wood, or oil, it can also be creative content in digital streams of music, literature, or movies. The goods that creative suppliers send into sales channels are more unique in content than other products, but also in their digital form very easy to reroute elsewhere. A commodity such as ten barrels of crude oil is replaceable with other barrels of same quality, but a particular creative product is not a direct substitute for another.

---

[95] Faulkender and Yang (2013).

On the other hand, the physicality and replace-ability of regular commodities makes them less fleeting, once they are packed and shipped. Creative content can therefore be both easier and harder to source without interruption. The following appeal was written by a music portal executive, to its main suppliers, i.e., musicians:

> "Here's the thing I really want artists to understand: Our interests are totally aligned with yours. Even if you don't believe that's our goal, look at our business. Our whole business is to maximize the value of your music. We don't use music to drive sales of hardware or software. We use music to get people to pay for music. The more we grow, the more we'll pay you. We're going to be transparent about it all the way through".

> Daniel Ek, CEO, Spotify[96]

Regardless of how Spotify succeeds with that appeal, I think the quote displays several of the characteristics

---

[96] Quoted from company website as found on November 11, 2014 on https://news.spotify.com/se/2014/11/11/2-billion-and-counting/

of resourcing challenges that all businesses eventually will face, and which will increasingly push firms towards adopting an *Open Resourcing* principle.

I firmly believe that people will voluntarily share in responsibilities, the more insight they have into the present situation, and the better view they have of the whole picture, and therefore detect themselves where it is meaningful to put in efforts, and see the reasonable sourcing costs from all viewpoints.

By understanding as much as possible about the corporation and its current and upcoming allocations for delivery capacity, the easier it is to find ways to contribute, and also to accept the ongoing of everything else. No-one can be commanded into motivation, but control structures can always be improved to make motivation more likely.

12

Energize with Honesty

Executing the Glass Cube Strategy has a major implementation theme: "Energize with Honesty". This theme accents the importance of completely honest communication across the cubic dimensions of enterprise:

- about the real customer value of the products (or lack of value if they fail to deliver on promised benefits)

- about the actual status of operations at every moment

- about what the resources are and exactly where they came from

In all three dimensions, organizational energy is added via the ruthless dropping of acts and relentless pushing for truth.

Strategy execution also includes the never-ending effort of re-inventing the strategic content; ongoing re-positioning in the Glass Cube, tirelessly shifting its internal organization of prisms to achieve better results in all dimensions, and visualizing these dynamics as events are planned and unfold.

In this dynamic visualization, it is manifest that there should be many rays to shine on parts of the cube that are performing at or near the most vital delivery points, and where attention is rightly high.

As a consequence, it is also perfectly normal to allow less glare in the parts that are reasonably internal, e.g. for staff training purposes (where the trainee can relax in making some failures only for discussion with the instructor), or for some laboratory experiments (with details that are premature to discuss publicly). Even so, the process statistics of such training and such laboratory work are still made viewable at a reasonable level.

In other words, the transparency of a Glass Cube is not to be thought of as an on/off property of the whole cube or of every internal prism, no matter from which viewpoint and angle, but more like a property of gradient translucency, causing some reasonable refractions depending on one's current viewpoint.

This optical effect as natural part of the metaphor is in fact there to make it easier to interact with, and inspect, the particular part that really needs to be seen most clearly at a particular situation, in a specific role, or as an external stakeholder. Information overload is not beneficial in itself.

It does not mean that internal shapes will still remain invisible, when one has more time to inspect the next level and simply moves ones current viewpoint a little bit, or in a an adjacent role need more insight, or if there is concern that something is not well.

To make this analogy more plain; say for instance that a customer may want to read about some main product properties, and will therefore have easy opportunities to do so, without being obstructed with irrelevant status data about, e.g., a training seminar last year on administrative routines for newly recruited staff, or some other facts, that are non-secret but so much less important from that angle. The refraction of light from the cube, is from that angle just a helpful filter effect. It is about usability and friendly encounter, more than anything else.

Sometimes, the lack of complete transparency in a prism is there only to safe-guard the necessary privacy of involved persons as private individuals, as previously discussed. Such calibration only shows that the Glass Cube Strategy is implemented appropriately.

Again, execution of the Glass Cube Strategy is primarily about persevering in communicating about the corporation in all the cubic dimensions of enterprise all the time and over time, i.e. utilizing the Glass Cube metaphor, concepts that are very abstract, but still must be spoken about in a very factual way, and with brutal honesty.

Business units and business areas are prisms within the cube, and these change according to circumstances and strategic execution. When animating the progress through time, the effects from one viewpoint can be quite kaleidoscopic.

Describing the movement of the Glass Cube through time is what Drucker called the "time dimension of management"[97]. This completeness of the picture and the visualization into animated progress, together with the radical honesty disseminating throughout the cube, sweeping out rumors and misconceptions, will turn into the motivational energy so

---

[97] Drucker (1954)

dearly needed for defending, continuing, and developing the business.

In this way, the continuously improved language, with an incessantly refined and deepened vocabulary used for coordinating and developing the corporation, becomes in itself a strategic thrust forward.

Principle 8: Safeguard Privacy

As mentioned in chapter 4, management has a distinct responsibility to defend employees right to privacy, not only in the moment, but also for the future. Open Operations Status does not mean that burglars can call the office, and ask when the employee will be home. Open Resourcing does not mean that a citizen can email to the police department demanding the roll call for today's patrol cars, or that a supermarket manager will display a website to give you your favorite cashier for the upcoming weekend shopping. A parent must let the headmaster of a school decide the allocation of teachers for next year, and a colleague must not necessarily know which courses another colleague was applying for two years ago but was declined at that point. Just because data is available, does not mean that it is strategically important to disclose, and the privacy cost may well exceed any other minor benefit of disclosure. Then, the principle of *Safeguard Privacy* should overrule.

«»

Let me take another example where *Safeguard Privacy* can overrule openness. With the rising amount of promotional statements and media clips on intranet and websites, and the currently expanding employer branding activities, permanent digital archiving is often a disregarded phenomenon. If an ex-employee does no longer want to be part of an infomercial video advertisement while no longer working for the company, will that particular clip within a video library where the ex-employee features, be deleted, or at least de-activated from promoted public publishing? Will such deletion require an active formal request and a manual effort, or is it automated thanks to a standardized part in the off-boarding routines? Will the deletion routine be different depending on which title the ex-employee had? If a role in the line organization is instated with expectation of external media involution, it should be part of the job description. For everyone else, involvement must be completely optional, without giving any reason for declining a particular publishment. Obviously, there is also the ongoing weaving of social networks, that has not yet fully stabilized a global netiquette. It is hardly necessary to quickly link up all job-acquaintances on all social networks, into the same webs as with all friends and one's entire family. Although a youthful positive attitude is a norm in most contemporary workplaces, one may pause and accept that apps that were designed for college students for fun, may not have to be fully applicable in every part of life for everyone all the time.

«»

A bigger problem area in this discussion, because of its well-intended aura, is the "wellness syndrome"[98]. This is the constantly rising expectation, that the overall

---

[98] An excellent review of the book by Cederström and Spicer with that title is McLemee (2015).

positive attitude is expected to combine with physical fitness, to design an ideal employee. The syndrome refers to the strain of responding to the multitude of wellness ideals and success displays, into a perfect recipe for chronic anxiety. The "wellness syndrome" is spreading both as part of benefit packages, but more so as informal norms on off-duty achievements and regarding acceptable absence from work. Actually, it is not so evident from statistics that overly allowing all employees to go and exercise while on paid duty, would be always economically correct policy to apply as a general rule for all workplaces everywhere. Therefore, it looks more like these programs are being intro-duced as a moral imposition[99].

If an employer wants to give all employees an hour a day for personal development, that is fine, and then it should not matter if that break is spent walking

---

[99] A study performed by RAND corporation for the U.S. Depart-ment of Labor and the U.S. Department of Health and Human Services, showed that wellness programs had little effect on employer total spending on health care. See: Mattke, et al. (2013). In an adjacent study, Mattke et al. (2014) , they found that employer return-on-investment (ROI) on health programs were very different in their two main component: 380% for disease management, but -50% for lifestyle management. That would indicate that employers are running lifestyle management subprograms for other reasons than business economics.

in the park, reading a book, doing some experimental programming, or maybe go out jogging. Some people can prefer take longer walk on Sunday afternoon instead of on a Monday morning, and that should be completely equal from a time compensation perspective.

The "wellness syndrome" is one of many tracks on a slippery slope where the integrity of employees as private individuals, is compromised. Some behaviors are highly respected at the water cooler, while others cause suspicion from colleagues, no matter if they are part of the duty time or not. However, a normal workplace is not future astronaut camp Gattaca, where employees are screened daily for medical data as they enter the building. The lion's share of employees around the world are first and foremost very normal people that should be allow to knit, play computer games, walk, jog, or whatever they like to do, when off-duty.

A commercial enterprise should have daily monitors of key performance indicators on many levels, and share these intensely with all staff. The blood pressure of an employee is not a corporate performance indicator, however important that data is for that particular individual's life and longevity. Apart for certain operator jobs that require health checks for safety reasons, there should be a separation between job supervision and health supervision. Workplaces where reasonable delimitation of supervision is not culturally instilled, will tend to have trouble also with other parts of the *Safeguard Privacy* principle.

«»

A final example of a situation where the *Safeguard Privacy* principle comes into play, is in so-called whistleblower programs[100]. In a democratic society, the interest of informed citizens via freedom of information acts[101], is subtly balanced against upkeeping of privacy, protecting legitimate business interests[102], and against explicitly secret details within core functions of the state. The whistleblower finds herself in the no man's land in between these sometimes fuzzy delimitations. Many things can be said about corporate whistleblower

---

[100] See Fox (1993) for introduction.

[101] For example, in the U.S. expressed in *5 U.S.C. § 552*, in Sweden expressed in *Tryckfrihetsförordning (1949:105)*. See also Gabriel (2009).

[102] Defined in national variations of business protection acts, for example in Sweden: *Lag (1990:409) om skydd för företagshemligheter*.

programs, the deeper problems behind them, and the results they may produce, but suffice to say that when those corporate programs exist, they are put in place to address special privacy concerns regarding the employer itself from its own employees, in a setting with critically conflicting goals are detected where the concept of loyalty (to whom and to what) has become a matter of profound disarray, and rising from a fear that a manager can overstep and shoot the messenger. The messenger is often primarily interested in having competent government and seeing honest business executives; that ethics should in general be inline with society as whole, but then the practical mess starts, and all the *sui generis* twilight.

Apart from ambitions of ethical business conduct and the negative brand impact consequences that a scandal brings, one reason why some corporations launch whistleblower programs is clearly that the opening of an internal investigation first can give the employer a chance to act on an upcoming concern before the activity becomes obviously criminal[103]. In comparison, a government investigation is a long and cost-

---

[103] A good analysis of communication channels for whistleblowers is Libit (2014).

ly process for the legal department to be involved in, hence the direct economic incentive to detect trouble earlier. This does not mean that an employee can be forced to contact the internal compliance program instead of the authorities.

Nevertheless, the typical employee may still prefer to quit, and leave the trouble behind, than take the personal risk and vocational burden to contact a compliance officer over an ethical dilemma. The potential payoff for engaging into a cause and becoming a whistleblower is often vague, and to take on that burden and new self-identity, is far from appetizing for most people. In the most difficult cases, the balancing line against treason is exceedingly thin.

I believe that the majority of whistleblowers, even the ones that overstep and commit espionage, have basically good intentions. They hit a moral conflict in an ugly reality and have received first-hand proof that the corruption is disgraceful and flagrant. But because the whistleblowers are alone in making their life-changing and career-impacting decisions, they can also easily be influenced by factors of vain, attention-seeking, desperation, and so on. In their action to disclose data, they can unintentionally expose some people that did not form the corrupted core of the problem, and by doing so, they can commit privacy faults themselves. A good whistleblower program will connect an anonymous caller to an independent advisory service to explore the options on how to minimize risks of espionage charges and libel, and how to present the data so that the criminality is laid bare, while simultaneously avoiding unnecessary damage to third parties. By invoking an advocate for documenting serious efforts made to try avoid wrongful acts against third party, it could probably reduce risks of malice (which includes the intent and will do to harm). Slander charges typically becomes more problematic for the whistleblower if any personal hatred could be suspected, there was a motive of ill will, and disregard of the interests of the person defamed. A whistleblower program should therefore assist in avoiding culpable recklessness. The whistleblower may feel the situation is black-and-white and the moral standpoint obvious, but the machinery of law has many wrinkles in the zone of overlapping civil and criminal law, and good advice can therefore be crucial.

It is absolutely in full accordance with Glass Cube Strategy, and a substantial counterpoint in implementing the *Safeguard Privacy* principle, that a corporation should as a minimum measure have an internal channel to vent concerns without fear of reprisals. Preferably, a whistleblower program should be set up according to best practices, with the interests of both the individual and the corporation aptly considered, and outside assistance involved as appropriate.

The loyalty conflicts and legal ramifications can be be utterly difficult in these matters, but luckily, most of us are spared from situations where it is a chief concern on a daily basis. So, we will move on to an easier principle now, within the major implementation theme "Energize with Honesty".

Principle 9: Closed Rehearsals

Managers and investors are crazy about metrics, it is an aptitude and job hazard, and I am sure they would be initially happy to get a current reading on absolutely anything in a business, from the average coffee break length of administrative assistants, to the average amount of gasoline used by a bus running hourly services between two stations. As we all know, some counts are easily manipulated into meaningless scores, e.g. the number of support tickets solved per day in a helpdesk call center, which is easy to double if each call is split into two parts and registered separately. Still, managers and their assistants can hardly resist counting anything that can be counted.

My forecast is that management reaction to any suggestions of increased transparency is initially positive, if they only understand it as receiving more real-time data on more things, without much effort to produce said data, or any direct costs arising. Sorry, that is of course not the case. It hardly means tighter control, either. In some areas, it may even imply giving the teams more space to maneuver on their own.

The trouble with overly monitoring in the name of efficiency, on metrics that are better kept more internal and subject to team coordination, is that the tracking efforts will cause side effects. The tracking seldom reduce cheating, but will effectively cause strong interference with ambitious employees' genuine efforts for improvement work and learning.

In most work nowadays, there needs to be an amount of slack, free time that is blocked out of people's time schedules, and used for experimentation, development, learning, recovery, and reflection. Chasing short-term profits by cutting back too much on this personal free float, even reducing it to zero, will look good temporarily but have negative impact on the medium- and long term.

In academics, there are so-called sabbaticals, periods of time where no output is forced. In some technology companies there are some explicitly free time given to experiment, without demand on any guaranteed outcome. Operators of complex machinery, can be given extra simulator sessions for serious play, where especially difficult and unusual scenaria can be practiced in sandbox setups without hazard of injury.

Too *much* visibility in *every* part of operations at all times, cause self-conscious inhibitions[104]. The more complex the tasks and the higher the expectations on teamwork, the more practice is needed before meeting the customer or engaging in the production line. To achieve great quality in performance mode, one needs ample room first, where errors will be made and learned from, gradually increasing the skills towards the required level. In whatever role, instructor feedback on training missions or simulator sessions can be kept much more offline, than data on core production

---

[104] Bernstein (2014)

processes. Although work in the field (action learning) is arguably the most powerful learning environment, the training period better not involve customers too soon. Young pilot cadets are obviously not beginning their aviation career by taking off in an A380 with seven hundred passengers into hard weather towards an unknown airport, to see how that goes, without even having made one single landing in a small airplane by themselves before.

Long hours of rehearsal is of course also why musicians and theater actors will perform well in front of an audience, but only after had ample space of important privacy with enough time to practice first (completely alone, or with colleagues and trusted instructors).

Corporations with tough profit targets and ambitious transparency policies, also need to understand that, sometimes, there still needs to be a sign on the door that says "rehearsal in progress".

Principle 10: Realtime Re-Alignment

The measurements displayed in accordance with the Open Operations Status principle, should be set up so that they enforce equality with the other axes. This means that deliveries in the product dimension can not exceed fulfillment capacity from operations. In the same manner, operations cannot draw more resources than are actually made available (in one way or the other).

In geometrical terms, such ruptures would mean that the cube lost its necessary compactness. At each point in time, all prisms within the cube, as well as the cube as a whole need to be aligned to the same and correct facts; the measurements must show what is happening for real. The activities in the Operations dimension can not detach from the sourcing from the Resources dimension, and so on.

It does not mean that everything is executing idealistically and according to plans. Things never are! The principle just states that the measurements are correct, and that they add up.

Also, re-aligning to reality does not mean that all activities are aligned with previously set strategic goals; the principle enforces that agile reallocations are being executed correctly. No one benefits from having resources locked into unproductive settings only because it was the previous plan. Plans need to change all the time, and then, allocation sheets must be realigned instantly.

Some well-known examples, when execution of previous plans did not pan out as expected, are:

- Delivery delays where a backlog of sold products is occurring because fulfillment is not able to keep up. The reasons for the delay can be internal or external factors, or combinations of both. Of course, delivery completion is not only concerning shipment of physical produce. A mission or service task that is late to complete in accordance with customer expectation and is binding resources longer than planned, is a form of delivery delay.

- Resources are overallocated to work more in operations than normally. Such overallocation (overtime work, or exceeding normal production ranges) must still be feasible and currently occurring in real life in the corporation, the overallocation that enforce alignment means to source more, at more cost or risk; it is not a fictional way to make the axes align within a planning tool only.

- Short-cuts are taken to avoid delays or overal-locations, leading to delivery quality impact, and the promised customer value is not generated.

The above examples of realignment needs, are probably the three most common and problematic operational misalignments within a running business.

In contrast, planned under-utilization of a resource is normally not a serious rupture against the principle of *Realtime Re-Alignment* , as long as slack resources are listed properly in the intersection between Resources and Operations, and the slack is booked as such. The obvious problem with severe under-utilization is of course that it degrades profitability. So, if not intentional and calibrated properly, too much slack resources will quickly become a major threat to corporate survival.

Not re-aligning with facts is not an option. No matter how bad some news are or how discouraging some data might be. In 1996, Jim Collins with research team started to investigate how a good company can become a great company[105]. One of their main discoveries was that a vision for greatness was not enough: the success-

---

[105] Collins (2001)

ful companies kept refining their path to greatness by continuously confronting brutal facts, however depressing they can be at the moment. Collins dubbed this "the Stockdale Paradox":

> "You must never confuse faith that you will prevail in the end - which you can never afford to lose - with the discipline to confront the most brutal facts of your current reality, whatever they might be."

> Admiral James Stockdale[106], quoted in Collins (2001).

After some practice, the workforce will take pride in confronting with facts, sharing decisions, weaknesses and strengths.

I have noticed that some professionals hoard information and then reveal it only in the moment when it makes them look good, politically. This is not in accordance with Glass Cube Strategy. To state one's thoughts immediately, or as soon as practical, is part of the major implementation theme "Energize with Hon-

---

[106] Stockdale survived eight years in prison during the Vietnam War, while many other soldiers died around him in the harsh imprisonment, where sheer optimism was not helpful.

esty". Someone who do not share early in the decision process, dramatizing the effect for a later revelation, is only selfish.

In practical use, the principle of *Realtime Re-Alignment* is working tight conjunction with the parallel principles of *Open Operations Status* and *Open Books*. Although (near) real-time realignment is the goal, additional post-facto analysis is also possible as part of the principle of *Open Operations Archives*.   But management can not steer well by looking in a rear-view mirror (and the workforce and the customers will detect if there are serious delays in the information flows). That's why all realignment with facts needs to be as imminent to the action as possible. A central task for Internal IT is to work on connecting all the data pipes (and they are many) for practical and successful adherence to the principles of *Open Operations Status, Open Books,* and *Realtime Re-Alignment.*

13

Conclusion

Meaningful Work

We can think of conventional management residing in a flat land full of frustrating situations where ordered activities often lead to slightly disappointing outcomes. Implementing the Glass Cube Strategy means encouraging a four-dimensional symbolic view of causalities in the three-dimensional organization as it passes through time; a complex interaction where intended outcomes for Products draw activities in Operations using the appropriate Resources. Those activities also trim internal alignments, reinforce learning, and even affect the beliefs among human resources that are involved.

Operational activities launch a myriad of calibrations within the cube, that justify and interpret actual outcomes, which leads to new ideas for improved outcomes in the next rounds. The conflicts that naturally occur in while managing along different axes in the Glass Cube, are brought into visibility as translucent prisms. These prisms are to be constantly discussed as abstractions, and are not personal power empires. Only if there is widespread doubt about the purpose of the organization and about the chosen strategy, there will be room for ruthless power as a way out of conflicting goals. Mere power struggle only degenerates the resource base.

So instead of drawing political blood, expected conflicts must be culturally guided into a mutual recalibration energy for the ever-changing organization on the ongoing journey. Suggestions that are not rational do not acquire automatic support: all proposals need sound base. Resisting ungrounded or diverting tangents can be necessary to safeguard an ongoing delivery, and everyone has different roles in tracking and securing different parts.

Safeguarding particular items as necessary for responsibility, does not imply an overall negativity to everything at all times. Leaning in and participating in changes, while viewing the ongoing transformations from as many angles as possible, becomes immensely more interesting than the alternative of accepting one frozen historic image from just one viewpoint, thereafter only grinding on one designated spot, defending it against all internal enemies.

By participating in improved expression about and visualizations of an allocation sheet, a prism such as a business unit, a cube, a family of cubes, or giant sectors of enterprise space with thousands of cubes, we transcend our role as a resource or stakeholder, and engage in a wider view on events.

A person acting in one role, defends some assigned aspect, at one point in time. Another person works on other angles. Over the next months, roles can be inverted, and be on another subject. A cornerstone in Glass Cube Strategy is to put the abstract prisms as objects separate from the persons working, and make the abstract objects into neutral facts to discuss. The prisms do not have feelings, motivation, or concerns. People who engage in work can have those things, and feed their energy into their work. The glass is cold, but the people talking about it can be passionate.

All that matters while working together in this modern form of organization, is the shared respect for the general development stream, and that it takes more than one person, perhaps even many teams, to tango.

Progress, adaptations, or even standstills, when done properly, all become exciting, beautiful, and full of meaning[107].

This is how good strategy generates organizational energy, so that the reinforcement learning loop becomes a positive and forward-thrusting experience. Hence, we approach reaching full circle in this book, by looking at the three strategic questions again, one last time.

---

[107] Looking at the events in this way is part of the Symbolic Approach according to Bolman and Deal (1984).

Answering the first strategic question

Because enterprise space is vast, a general business strategy can not spell out the *verbatim* answer to the first strategic question (what products a particular corporation should offer). Implementing Glass Cube Strategy is chiefly concerned with *how* the first strategic question is answered, then re-answered, again and again. This includes the challenge of truthfully visualizing the product axis according to customer benefit valuation, as clearly as possible.

From this follows that all stakeholders will have good insight on the decision processes: the setup of product platforms, current specifications on all the products, and the product roadmaps. The most radical disclosures are perhaps the ones on measurements of customer benefits as a whole, and the internal assessment of platform contribution and attributions to each product. Building a strong product range from a clever platform, is a product strategy to be genuinely proud of, not a secret sauce added behind the scenes.

The corporation has made assumptions about customer benefits, and therefore invested accordingly. The next step is to present these assumptions as lucidly as possible, so that presumptive and current customers can easily check and then concur or disagree with that analysis. Compromises are always made in product design, if non-obvious compromises was made, they should be explained. Points where a competitor can be stronger for a particular customer segment are not to be hidden under the carpet, but acknowledged as matter-of-fact. From all this material, it will be evident why the corporation is offering exactly what it is offering, and not something else.

The honesty in the product appraisal will reinforce the sense of validity in the information. This strategy can even lead to sales or retention even in non-targeted segments, even if competitors have been given due credit, even praise, simply because some customers prefer a supplier that sees the world in the way presented, appreciate that respect was shown when relevant, and like how the product line analysis was presented.

Product data in this context is not only a folder with static specification sheets, it is also many ongoing snapshots and trend analysis of both visible and invisible production qualities, and various usage statistics that are measured frequently for products in use. Similarly, the facts about product returns or service complaints are occurrences in the delivery process, and can therefore not be neglected. Or worse, cause a spin control theater where reality warping is trying to divert the negative attention, and is drawing more creativity and efforts, than the energy spent on striving for actually useful product and service qualities; the worst cases in this category being more or less elaborate scams.

Disclosure will be very uncomfortable at first: -'Will the competition study this rich product information that is constantly presented?' -'Yes, they definitely should'. -'Does that mean the data should better be hidden out of view for everyone, for as long as possible?' -'No, absolutely not'.

So, implementing Glass Cube Strategy is putting the pressure on the *way* the answer to the first strategic questions is to be formulated: in a dialogue fashion. The dialogue is continually presented and updated, with breathtaking openness about the underlying analysis for the offerings, and on the measured or assessed customer benefits.

The answer to the first strategic question is discovered, rehearsed, and repeated in a forever ongoing discussion with stakeholders. The focus in the dialogue is on benefits in genuine deliveries; not as virtual fluff in soft speech or glossy marketing, but factually and to the point, in the crisp air of harsh reality.

Answering the second strategic question

Glass Cube Strategy gives a hint to the answer on the second strategic question (on how to differentiate in the way to create value). First, the analysis on customer benefits must be correct, so that can not happen if hiding out of view. Then a product platform strategy can give the needed leverage to the product line. As noted above in the paragraph on product strategy openness, it is a differentiating thrust in having a befitting and well-serving operational transparency on product design and product delivery, that builds trust with all stakeholders. Not only monthly sales figures, but long-term confidence levels are crucial. A good sign of confidence is if the current workforce as well as the alumni are proud of the product calibrations made for the best interest of the customers, and if all customers signed up by their free and intentional will and if they are consistently content that promises were delivered upon. This search, and re-calibration of value vectoring, is evidently not a once-off action, but an ongoing work of following the principles as outlined in the previous chapters.

Answering the third strategic question

The hard efforts described above, can not diminish when the path goes uphill. There will be many struggles and plenty temptations to start protective shutdowns of communication, copious opportunities to give up on all previously set ambitions of openness.

So, above and beyond merely sourcing the particular resources needed for operations on a particular day, a distinct capability, one that is essential for successful differentiation, is the compelling conviction of adhering to the principles of the Glass Cube Strategy, even when it is hard.

Repeating these efforts enough times, not least while performing extra difficult or temporarily impopular tasks, makes them become part of organizational culture, and then they can start to reinforce themselves. When it has become part of the special competencies of the organization to openly and vigilantly press ahead even in headwind, successfully mustering the resources needed to keep delivering the best product possible, and showing integrity whatever the circumstance, then by doing so, as a consequence, the corporation will earn and upkeep the trust of customers, workforce, partners and investors alike.

No matter in which industry or geography, *trustworthiness* - by successful, qualitative product deliveries in the chosen field, thanks to proper resourcing and partner cooperation, and operating with a transparent attitude in all three dimensions of enterprise – emerges as the general resolution on the single capability most needed to persistently and fruitfully differentiate as a business.

Achievement of trustworthiness is not the sporadic result of a once-off commendation by management, but a continual quality judgment made by stakeholders, every hour, every day. It requires an enormously stubborn effort to build, and all human resources involved must help to their best ability, or it is simply not going to come about.

Radical Responsibility

After lifting unnecessary veils of secrecy within and around the corporation, and beginning radically share information, there is not supposed to be overly diffusing accountability into an anarchy where no one is to answer for anything. Executing Glass Cube Strategy implies reorganizing responsibility over information flows so that more people in the organization are involved and actually expected to act prudently.

The old-fashioned style of accountability puts individuals as lone rangers, cheering those that manage to chase off trouble, and pursuing the person who took the one wrong decision in hindsight. What about all the input and corrections that should have been available before that decision? People can not stop taking decisions, to avoid the wrong decisions. Very few insider criminals succeed without an amount of passivity surrounding them. The passivity of the surrounding organization is often also culprit to the crime. That is why it is safer to have all people that are involved to also be looking out for strange facts or missing data.

Trained helplessness is draining any organization of thrust. To keep moving, decisions need to be made.

All decisions are to be taken when they need to be taken, on the base that are available at that time. That is the best to hope for. The responsibility included in each role is to do as much as possible to clarify the decision base at the moment, for oneself and for connected roles upstream and downstream. Producers of decision data are also consumers of similar data, readers are also authors, and persons in the workforce act in several roles in parallel. Increased openness is therefore not so much upgrading an existing one-way alley into a slightly wider one, but to open many new two-way streets, and work hard to remove roadblocks that is hindering the flow of real-time information.

That more facts and circumstance that people can see of what is happening within and around a corporation, the more purposeful the thousands of daily decisions will be. The privilege of a better view, comes with an obligation to redistribute data wisely, seek task-relevant information,   show decency with cooperating roles, and help build good, professional etiquette.

Business leaders need to hear any bad news just as timely as the good news, in fact, preferably faster. This means that not informing about trouble, is worse than speaking up, and alerting potentially dangerous situations. Putting pressure on people that they all should always be flexible and positive and say yes, also when saying no would have been more the more responsible thing to do, will not foster a good culture for long-term success. 'Look out!' can sometimes be the nicest thing anyone can shout to you.

In continuously reinventing the organization, adapting the capacity and allocations to be able to deliver useful products, the people involved are not the same as their roles, accountability is not only in hierarchies, and everyone participating needs quick access to good visualization tools to see what is happening at the moment. The roles are in a constant flux, but in every moment they are fixed. The corporation is not a machine that is being trimmed by men in white coats, neither is it an exotic organism with a will of its own. A corporation is merely an abstraction of intents in the three dimensions of enterprise, and the Glass Cube can be a befitting metaphor for amalgamating data on the decisions and events while progressing in that space, making it easier to keep the topic on track.

If the workforce, with insight in the production, are not proud of the deliveries, why would a customer like it? Other stakeholders also have a particular stewardship. An owner is making a statement every day to remain invested in a corporation, and must therefore also be content that all the efforts being made, are producing customer value. In fact, the duty of *all* persons involved in a corporation is to keep reflecting upon what the expectations in their current role imply, in relation to what the actual situation is at the moment. Moreover, to help interpreting and clarifying the situation at hand, and the outlook from the available viewpoint. What is the bold thing to do? What is the safe and proud thing to do?

No matter how much machinery is installed, or how much money is invested, the most critical and irreplaceable constituents when aspiring to build a trustworthy enterprise, are good people with high integrity.

They need to hold the various prisms of the Glass Cube in their steady hands, put their minds together to view it all, and stay curious to see how the story will continue.

References

Agan, T. (2014). "Please Stop Ideating". Harvard Business Review, April, 2014. Retrieved January 30, 2015, from https://hbr.org/2014/04/please-stop-ideating

Aho, A. V., Sethi, R., and Ullman, J. D. (1986). Compilers, principles, techniques, and tools. Reading, MA. Addison-Wesley Pub.

Almazan, A., Suarez, J., and Titman, S. (2007). "Firms' Stakeholders and the Costs of Transparency". National Bureau of Economic Research Working Paper No. 13647, November 2007.

Anderson, C. (2006). "In Praise of Radical Transparency". Wired Blog. Retrieved November 4, 2014 from www.longtail.com/the_long_tail/2006/11/in_praise_of_ra.html

Argyris, C. (1990). Overcoming Organizational Defenses. Facilitating Organizational Learning. Boston. Allyn & Bacon.

Aurik, J., Fabel, F., and Jonk, G. (2014). "The History of Strategy and Its Future Prospects". A.T. Kearny Ideas and Insights. Retrieved December 8, 2014 from http://www.atkearney.com/strategy/futureproof-strategy/

Aurik, J., Fabel, F., and Jonk, G. (2014). "The State of Strategy Today - Findings in A.T. Kearney's 2014 Strategy Study". A.T. Kearny Ideas and Insights. Retrieved December 8, 2014 from http://www.atkearney.com/strategy/futureproof-strategy/

Austin, D.A., and Gravelle, J.G. (2008). Does Price Transparency Improve Market Efficiency? Implications of Empirical Evidence in Other Markets for the Health Sector. Congressional Research Service RL34101. Retrieved January 14, 2015 from http://fas.org/sgp/crs/misc/RL34101.pdf

Ben-Shahar, O., and Schneider, C.E. (2014). More than you wanted to know. the failure of mandated disclosure. Princeton University Press.

Bernstein, E. (2014). "The Transparency Trap". Harvard Business Review, October 2014.

Bolman, L.G., and Deal, T.E. (1984). Modern Approaches to Understanding and Managing Organizations. Jossey-Bass Limited.

Brockman, G. (2014). "Scaling email transparency". Stripe blog, December 8, 2014. Retrieved February 2, 2015 from https://stripe.com/blog/scaling-email-transparency

Camfferman, K. and Zeff, S.A. (2003). "The apotheosis of holding company accounting: Unilever's financial reporting innovations from the 1920s to the 1940s". In Accounting, Business & Financial History 13:2 July 2003 171–206. Taylor & Francis Ltd.

Cheynel, E. (2013). "A theory of voluntary disclosure and cost of capital". Review of Accounting Studies. December 2013, Volume 18, Issue 4, pp 987-1020.

Cleden, D. (2012). Managing Project Uncertainty (Advances in Project Management). Gower Publishing, Ltd., September 28, 2012.

Collins, J. (2001). Good to Great: Why Some Companies Make the Leap... and Others Don't. Random House Business Books, London.

Coughlan, A.T. (2013). "The Elephant in the Room: The Benefits of Creative Destruction in Airline Distribution". Kellogg School of Management, Northwestern University. Presented at IATA World Passenger Symposium 2014. Retrieved January 14, 2015 from http://www.iata.org/events/passenger-symposium/

Croft, J. (2015). "Can Global Surveillance Be Crowd-Sourced?". Aviation Week & Space Technology, Mar 17, 2015.

Das, D.K. (ed.) (2011). Strategic Alliances for Value Creation. Information Age Publishing Inc.

Dichter, G. S., Felder, J. N., Green, S. R., Rittenberg, A. M., Sasson, N. J., and Bodfish, J. W. (2012). "Reward circuitry function in autism spectrum disorders". Social Cognitive and Affective Neuroscience, 7(2), 160–172. Retrieved January 14, 2015 from doi:10.1093/scan/nsq095

Doty, E. (2014). "Integrity is Free". strategy+business blog December 16, 2014. Columbia Business School. Retrieved October 14, 2015, from http://www.strategy-business.com/blog/Integrity-is-Free?gko=d3089

Drucker, P.F. (1954). The Practice of Management. Reprint 2010. Harper Collins.

Falkenberg, K. (2010). "Disclosed to Death". Forbes Magazine 2010/0607. Retrieved December 4, 2014, from http://www.forbes.com/

Faulkender, M. and Yang, J. (2013). "Is Disclosure an Effective Cleansing Mechanism? The Dynamics of Compensation Peer Benchmarking". The Review of Financial Studies. 26 (3): 806-839.

Fox, R.G. (1993). "Protecting the Whistleblower". Adelaide Law Review v.15, no. 2, pp.137-163. Retrieved November 30, 2015 from http://www.austlii.edu.au/au/journals/AdelLawRw/1993/6.pdf

Fung, A., Graham. M., Weil, D. (2008). Full Disclosure: The Perils and Promise of Transparency. Cambridge University Press.

Gabriel, M.C. (2009). "Plugging Leaks: The Necessity of Distinguishing Whistleblowers and Wrongdoers in the Free Flow of Information Act", 40 Loy. U. Chi. L. J. 531 (2009). Loyola University Chicago School Of Law. Available at: http://lawecommons.luc.edu/luclj/vol40/iss3/5

Gardner, L. (2012). "Should theatres open up their accounts?". Newspaper article in The Guardian, 7 February 2012. Retrieved January 14, 2015 from: http://www.theguardian.com/stage/theatreblog/2012/feb/07/fringe-theatre-open-accountable

Guiso, L., Sapienza, P., and Zingales, L., (2013). The Value of Corporate Culture. Chicago Booth Research Paper No. 13-80 (September 1, 2013); Fama-Miller Working Paper. Retrieved January 14, 2015 from: http://ssrn.com/abstract=2353486

Gulati, R. and Eppinger, S. (1996). The Coupling of Product Architecture and Organizational Structure Decisions. Massachusetts Institute of Technology Sloan School of Management Working Paper Number 3906.

Hinton, C.H. (1885). "Many Dimensions". Scientific Romances, Vol. 2, 1885. Reprinted in: Speculations on the Fourth Dimension, Selected Writings of Charles H. Hinton, 1980, by Dover Publications, Inc. Retrieved November 30, 2015 from: http://www.ibiblio.org/eldritch/chh/h4.html

Hinton, C.H. (1888). A new era of thought. London: Swan Sonnenschein & Co. Retrieved October 19, 2015 from: https://archive.org/details/cu31924068267602 (Book contributor Cornell University Library).

Hoffjan, A.H., Lührs, S., and Kolburg, A. (2011), Cost Transparency in Supply Chains: Demystification of the Cooperation Tenet (July 15, 2011). Schmalenbach Business Review, Vol. 63, pp. 230-251, July 2011. Available at SSRN: http://ssrn.com/abstract=1969408

IFAC (2013). "Project and Investment Appraisal for Sustainable Value Creation". International Good Practice Guidance. Professional Accountants in Business Committee, International Federation of Accountants. Retrieved January 30, 2015 from: http://www.ifac.org/publications-resources/project-and-investment-appraisal-sustainable-value-creation-1

Jarosinski, E. (2007). "Transparency: The Stranger in Our Midst". This Century's Review - journal for rational legal debate. Issue 01/07. Retrieved January 14, 2015 from: http://history.thiscenturysreview.com/transparencythest.html

Kafka, F. (1935). "The Trial" from Vintage Kafka - the complete novels. Vintage Books, London, 2008.

Lee, K. (2014). "The Advantages and Workflows of Fully Transparent Email". bufferopen blog, June 2014. Retrieved January 30, 2015, from: https://open.bufferapp.com/buffer-transparent-email/

Lemmergaard, J., Muhr, S.L. (Eds.). (2013). Critical perspectives on leadership. emotion, toxicity, and dysfunction. Cheltenham: Edward Elgar.

Libit, B., Draney, W., Freier, T. (2014). "Elements of an Effective Whistleblower Hotline". Harvard Law School Forum on Corporate Governance and Financial Regulation, October 25, 2014. Retrieved November 25, 2015, from: http://corpgov.law.harvard.edu/2014/10/25/elements-of-an-effective-whistleblower-hotline/

Lord, N. (2014). Regulating Corporate Bribery in International Business - Anti-corruption in the UK and Germany. Ashgate.

Macfarlane, A., and Martin, G. (2002). Glass: A World History. Chicago: University of Chicago Press.

Mackay, C. (1852). Memoirs of Extraordinary Popular Delusions and the Madness of Crowds. Vol.I. Office of the National Illustrated Library. Printed by Robson, Levey, and Franklyn.

Mattke S, Liu H, Caloyeras JP, Huang CY, Van Busum KR, Khodyakov D, and Shier V. (2013). "Workplace Wellness Programs Study:Final Report", Santa Monica, Calif. RAND Corporation, RR-254-DOL Retrieved November 25, 2015, from: at www.rand.org/t/RR254.

Mattke S., et al. (2014). "Do Workplace Wellness Programs Save Employers Money?". RAND Corporation, Research Brief RB-9744-DOL. Retrieved November 25, 2015, from: http://www.rand.org/pubs/research_briefs/RB9744.html.

McGee, R.C. (2004). My Adventure with Dwarfs: A Personal History in Mainframe Computers. University of Minnesota: Charles Babbage Institute. Retrieved January 1, 2015 from:

http://www.cbi.umn.edu/hostedpublications/pdf/McGe e_Book-4.2.2.pdf

McLemee, S. (2015) "Get Well Soon". Review of Carl Cederstrom and Andre Spicer 'The Wellness Syndrome'. Inside Higher Ed, May 6, 2015. Retrieved November 23, 2015 from: https://www.insidehighered.com/views/2015/05/06/re view-carl-cederstrom-and-andre-spicer-wellness-syndrome

Morgan, G. (2006). Images of organization. Thousand Oaks: Sage Publications.

Nobes, C., and Parker, R.H. (2008). Comparative International Accounting. Pearson Education.

Noda, T., and Bower, J.L (1996). "Strategy Making as Iterated Processes of Resource Allocation". Strategic Management Journal,Vol. 17, Special Issue: Evolutionary Perspectives on Strategy (Summer, 1996), pp. 159-192.

PwC (2010). "Achieving more timely, accurate and transparent reporting". Adisory Services Report, December 2010. PricewaterhouseCoopers LLP. Retrieved November 23, 2015 from: http://www.pwc.com/us/en/increasing-finance-function-effectiveness/publications/close-to-report.html

Rigby, D., and Bilodeau, B. (2007). "A Growing Focus on Preparedness". Harvard Business Review, July 2007. Retrieved January 19, 2015, from https://hbr.org/2007/07/a-growing-focus-on-preparedness

Sargent, R.L. (1927). "The Use of Slaves by the Athenians in Warfare". Classical Philology Vol. 22, No. 3 (Jul., 1927), pp. 264-279. Published by University of

Chicago Press. Retrieved October 23, 2015, from
http://www.jstor.org/stable/262754

Smith, R., and Tabibnia, G. (2012). "Why Radical
Transparency is Good Businesses". Retrieved October
8, 2015, from https://hbr.org/2012/10/why-radical-
transparency-is-good-business

Solove, D.J. (2007). 'I've Got Nothing to Hide' and Other
Misunderstandings of Privacy. San Diego Law Review,
Vol. 44, p. 745, 2007; George Washington University
Law School Public Law Research Paper No. 289.
Available at SSRN:http://ssrn.com/abstract=998565

Sundström, M. Raman (2010). "A pedagogical history of
compactness". (A condensed revised version of
Raman, M. (1997). Understanding Compactness: A
Historical Perspective. Masters of Arts Thesis.
University of California, Berkeley). Retrieved January
19, 2015, from arXiv:1006.4131v1

Thompson, C. (2007). "The See-Through CEO". Wired
magazine March 2007. Retrieved March 26, 2015,
from
http://archive.wired.com/wired/archive/15.04/wired40
_ceo.html#seven

Ticoll, D., and Tapscott, D. (2014). The Naked
Corporation: how the age of transparency will
revolutionize business. S.l.: Free Press.

Wagenhofer, A. (2007). "Economic Consequences of
Internet Financial Reporting". In New Dimensions of
Business Reporting and XBRL. Roger Debreceny,
Carsten Felden, Maciej Piechocki (eds.). Deutscher
Universitäts-Verlag, 2007.

Whitehead, A.N., and Russell, B. (1927). Principia
mathematica. Cambridge: Cambridge University Press.

Wittgenstein, L. (1953). Filosofiska undersökningar,
(transl. into Swedish by Wedberg, A.). Bonnier,

Stockholm, 1978. (First published 1953 as
Philosophical Investigations. Blackwell, Oxford).

Zaslow, J. "Surviving the Age of Humiliation". The Wall
Street Journal, May 5, 2010. Retrieved March 26, 2015
from: http://on.wsj.com/1s6Gu6x

ABOUT THE AUTHOR

David Lyback was born in Uppsala, studied at the Royal Institute of Technology and at Stockholm University. He has worked on financial software, many assignments in business analysis, and as management consultant specializing in strategy. He is married with three children.